NET RESULTS

NET RESULTS

TRAINING THE TENNIS
PARENT FOR COMPETITION

BY DR. JAMES E. LOEHR
AND E. J. KAHN III

THE STEPHEN GREENE PRESS

Lexington, Massachusetts

Copyright © The Stephen Greene Press, Inc., 1987
Foreword copyright © Nick Bollettieri, 1987

First published in 1987 by The Stephen Greene Press, Inc.
Published simultaneously in Canada by Penguin Books Canada Limited
Distributed by Viking Penguin Inc., 40 West 23rd Street, New York, NY 10010.

Photographs reproduced by permission of James Bollettieri.

Library of Congress Cataloging-in-Publication Data
Loehr, James E.
  Net results.

  1. Tennis for children—United States. 2. Parent and child—United States.
3. Tennis for children—United States—Psychological aspects. I. Kahn, E. J., 1947– . II. Title.
GV1001.4.C45L64 1987   796.342'024054   87-7583

ISBN 0-8289-0635-1
Designed by Lisa Bogle
Printed in the United States of America
by Haddon Craftsmen, Inc.
Set in Univers Condensed and Palatino
by Publication Services.
Produced by Unicorn Production Services, Inc.

To my youngest son, Jeff, as he enters competitive tennis — that I do as I say.   JL

To my wife, Rose, for keeping the pressure off.   EJK

CONTENTS

ACKNOWLEDGMENTS

This book is a true collaboration, not just of the authors, but of scores of friends and colleagues of the authors as well. Without their aid, counsel, and expertise, *Net Results* might still be a good idea awaiting execution.

Nick Bollettieri, who contributed this book's introduction, of course deserves our special thanks, as do the staff of the Bollettieri Academy. The United States Tennis Association, which has exhibited such keen interest in the book's research and conclusions, has been a strong supporter throughout this work. So have Head and Nike, two companies closely involved with the sport. And thanks, too, to the many competitors—both professional and amateur—who took the time to share their thoughts and experiences, which were invaluable.

Acknowledgments

Of course a special note of gratitude must go to the parents and coaches who talked with us. *Net Results* is not only written for them; in a very real sense, it has been written by them.

Among those the authors would specifically like to acknowledge for their help are: Jack Agnew; Neil Amdur; Arthur Ashe; Bill, Bonnie, and Cindy Barber; Ivan Blumberg; Vic Braden; Barbara Braunstein; Steve Casati; Tara Collins; Leif Dahlgren; Irv Dardik; Stephen Devereux; Michael Estep; Shawn Foltz; Bonnie Gadusek; Brian Gottfried; Jack Groppel; Tim and Rosemary Gullikson; Tom and Julie Gullikson; Tim Heckler; Diedre, Don, and Barbara Herman; Janet Heydt; Pat, Howard, Luke, and Murph Jensen; Joy Jodenberg; Eve Kraft; Aaron Krickstein; Dr. Herbert Krickstein; Robert Landsdorp; Ira Litke; Holly Lloyd; Clarence Mabry; Doug MacCurdy; Peter McLaughlin; Susan Mascarin; Ted Meekma; Alan Morell; Betsy Nagelsen; Fritz Nau; Greg Patton; Terry Phelps; Kathy Rinaldi; David Rosenbaum; Howard Schoenfield; Amy Schwartz; Steve Simons; Susan Sloane; Michelle Torres; Dennis Van der Meer; and Ron Woods.

Finally, our thanks to Thomas Begner, this book's publisher. Begner's a rare breed in publishing circles, understanding when to put the pressure on, and when to keep it off. And his love of the game, and commitment to it, shows in our work. Thanks, too, to our editor Rickie Harvey, whose perseverance has paid off.

FOREWORD

I have a confession to make.

My entire life has been involved in sport: as a partici-
pant, as a coach, as a spectator. Yet only in the past few
years has it become evident to me how much of competition is influenced by the mind. Yes, how a player hits his
forehand or prepares to return serve is important. But
there is so much more to the game of tennis than learning
how to hit a ball, so much below the game's surface, in the
player's mind.

Sports psychologist Jim Loehr, my colleague at the
Bollettieri Academy, helped me learn that revelatory lesson. And, with this book, he and coauthor E. J. Kahn III
bring those insights to the tennis public.

Junior tennis is an especially difficult sport for both parents and children. There is great pressure on the court—a fact that parents who've never played competitively often don't recognize. There is the considerable expense, which can put stress on families. There is the complicated relationship between the child and the teacher, the player and the coach, which can further strain the bonds between mother and father and son and daughter. For these reasons, and many more, it's important that parents be trained for competitive tennis, just as their children are.

This book is an excellent first step.

At the Bollettieri Academy, Jim Loehr's teaching led us to change aspects of our own training system. With Loehr's encouragement and guidance, we began to hold more group discussions, to give our players an opportunity to improve communication with the coaches and staff. We gave them more chances to talk about the problems they'd experienced and the anxieties they felt being away from home, about how to cope with stresses and pressure within their families, and about how to deal with those pressures on the court. We learned that young players away from home often feel isolated—literally out of touch—and we began a weekly massage program, giving the children a kind of surrogate physical contact that might compensate for the affectionate hugs they get at home. The students at the academy love the once-a-week sessions, and play better for them.

For our summer campers, too—children learning the game for the first time, without the goal of becoming ranked competitors—the influence of Jim Loehr has made a difference. The primary goal of these camps has always been to have fun, but Loehr has helped us to redefine and reemphasize its essential importance. Playing the sport should be fun for the child; if it isn't, then the experience is wrong.

Indeed, finding the winning in losing, giving all of yourself regardless of the outcome, is a principle in this book that is applicable to all sport. Sure, it's tough to lose. But, we've learned, it's trying hard that ultimately defines a player.

Unfortunately, parents often find that a difficult concept to accept. They refuse to perceive the complexity of the pressure their son or daughter is under. They measure success only by the final score. And that, realistically, reflects the American way of life. "You are who you beat." Yet that idea is beginning to change, at least in the world of tennis.

Junior tennis in America has the best talent in the world. If you take our top fifteen boys and top fifteen girls, no other country can beat us. Criticism about the quality of our players is, therefore, unwarranted. The talent is there.

Role models, on the other hand, are lacking. The top athletes in the sport don't accept the responsibilities that come with their stature and don't communicate a true love of the game to the masses. This country needs a new sense of fun about tennis, a broader, grass-roots approach that brings the sport into the schools and onto the playgrounds. Parents want that as much as the children: if their kids are turned off by the top players, the parents themselves will be hesitant about getting involved with the game.

This country is beginning to look at the European systems for guidance, and the United States Tennis Association (USTA) seems ready to establish some type of national junior center. Whether it will adopt a system of "super coaches," paid by the USTA to train top, selected juniors for national and international play, and whether there will be regional centers or one national center remain to be seen.

But change is in the air, and in my opinion, change can only make the insights of Jim Loehr even more relevant.

Jim Loehr's research and conclusions can help today's tennis parents determine if and when they've crossed the line and become problems themselves. Parents may use their children's tennis in ways that undercut the son or daughter's enjoyment and success—by looking at a ranking as a means of gaining social status or by treating a win–loss record as the bottom-line indicator on their financial investment. When that occurs, as Loehr and Kahn's book shows, parents grow critical of their children, forgetting their most important role: to be supportive, to be a positive influence.

Loehr and Kahn expand upon that most fundamental idea: parental love and understanding produce great tennis, winning tennis, at any level the young player competes. And that is a concept that applies to all junior sport, not simply tennis. For that reason, I hope this book finds a wide readership beyond the world of tennis.

Tennis parents, tennis coaches, administrators, officials—all can gain by perusing this work. It's a book, in the end, that addresses leadership. Leaders are independent and risk being ostracized. Yet by following their own paths, they emerge stronger, more able to handle pressure on and off the court. Trained tennis parents will serve as leaders, both for their child and for the sport. And this book offers those important lessons.

The Bollettieri Academy has been fortunate to have Jim Loehr on its staff and to be able to provide the facilities for his research and work and to help him find his audience in the tennis world. With this book, that audience should expand dramatically.

—Nick Bollettieri

NET RESULTS

PROLOGUE

Like every other tennis parent at the Zoo, Pat Jensen was feeling the pressure. Unlike the others, she was freaking out over the absence of a four-foot promotional gimmick.

Here they were, more than 24 hours into the 1986 United States Tennis Association Boys' 18 and 16 National Championships, and the forty-eight-inch-tall graphite tennis racquet wasn't on display. It wasn't, in fact, even on the grounds of Kalamazoo College, the pristine western Michigan campus where the premier junior tennis tournament in the country—nicknamed the Zoo for its site—had been played since 1943.

Didn't anybody understand? thought Jensen, the mother of four nationally ranked boys and girls. Jack Sullivan, the president of a Princeton, New Jersey, racquet company, would be arriving the next day. His firm out-fitted nearly 50 percent of the more than 275 players at the championships, supplying at no cost hundreds of racquets that retailed for more than $100 apiece. Sullivan's company had set up a temporary pro shop to service those players and their racquets. The company was providing free stringing, free hats, free equipment bags, free headbands, even free advice. "Why don't you stencil your racquet?" the company representative said sweetly, but firmly, to juniors whose strings lacked the company's logo. "You look naked out there during your match."

"Get over to my house, and get that racquet," shouted Jensen, finally collaring a young volunteer who looked barely old enough to drive. "No ifs, ands, or buts."

"See," Jensen said, turning to the representative, "I'm doing your job for you."

As if Pat Jensen didn't have enough to worry about. One year ago, her oldest son, Luke, had won the 18-and-under championship and had ended the year ranked number one in the world in his age group. After a court-ship that included most of the top tennis colleges in the country, he'd accepted a four-year scholarship to the University of Southern California. While Pat Jensen was retrieving the oversized racquet, Luke was in Raleigh, North Carolina, playing in a small professional satellite tournament.

Luke's younger brother, Murphy, a gangly, blond 17-year-old, was with his mother — and father — in Kalamazoo. Murphy was seeded twelfth in the singles and first in the doubles, where he was paired with Al Parker, a Georgian who was the top seed in the singles. Murphy was the highest-seeded local boy, and his results were followed by most of the Michigan papers. Although the Jensen children had been born and raised in Ludington, a resort town on the shore of Lake Michigan, Pat and Murphy had moved two years before the tournament to Grand Rapids, an aging city just an hour from Kalamazoo by expressway. Luke had left Ludington for that city two years before that. But now, with Luke out of the juniors, Murphy was southern Michigan's favorite son.

When Pat and the boys moved to Grand Rapids, father Howard Jensen had stayed behind with the twin girls, Rachel and Rebecca. For more than a decade, Howard had coached tennis at Ludington High School, and he had deep roots in the community. What began as a favor to the local principal—in his first year with the team, he knew so little about choosing a lineup for a match that he determined who'd play in the first five slots by staging a four-mile run; the winner got to play the opposition's best—had become a commitment. Normally, he would have been with the 13-year-old girls down south, where they were playing a national 14-and-under tournament. But Howard Jensen, whose bald head and trim physique gave him the appearance of a grizzled football lineman (which he in fact had been, on one of coach Ray Malavasi's University of Minnesota teams), decided instead to stay close to home and watch Murphy.

Murphy Jensen had had a good season, his first in the 18s, but not—in the eyes of the USTA—good enough. Unlike his brother the year before, Murphy Jensen had not been named to the USTA's Junior Davis Cup team, an elite group that got special clothing, intensive training, subsidized travel, and entry into selected professional events. "They accused Murphy of dodging tournaments," said Pat Jensen, "which is ridiculous."

Murphy, Pat felt, had something to prove at Kalamazoo.

The time spent in the stands, or on the sidelines, had become the Jensens' equivalent of leisure. In Pat Jensen's lap sat a large vinyl notebook bulging with scraps of paper. Its cover read "Five Year Planner," but Pat called it her "Five Minute Planner." Inside were phone numbers, appointments, and notes on negotiations. "I work six to eight jobs," Pat would say, handing out business cards that described her as a promoter of special events. Racquet stringing, clothing design, tennis camp management—the Jensens had grown proficient at all. A 1979 van the family would use to haul players to and from tournaments had passed the 300,000-mile mark on the odometer, and three engines had come and gone. "My friends would accuse me of changing motors, not oil," Pat would say with a grin.

Every weekend, the Jensens would hit the road, either to compete or to practice. Yet Pat wasn't complaining. Not a bit. The parents of nationally ranked junior players had to sacrifice. There was no choice. In making those commitments, Pat Jensen felt, a family grew stronger.

"Every time we need money for plane tickets," Pat said, "I pray to the good Lord. And every time, I get a job for just the right amount of money. There's never any left over either. But the strength of our family doesn't come from what we make or win, it comes from our pulling for each other."

Because Prince was pulling for the Jensens, too—the company's investment in the four juniors over the years amounted to thousands of dollars—Pat wanted to make sure everything was just right for the sponsor. She'd learned, through her own promotions, the importance of that. To be on the Prince equipment list—or Head's or Nike's—was a high honor, reserved for members of the elite. Unless you were among the top 45 players in the country in your age group, the company normally wouldn't consider you. To some kids, making an equipment manufacturer's list was as important as making the draw at the Zoo. Doing Prince a favor in return, figured Jensen, couldn't hurt.

"There's a lot of intensity out there," observed Dr. Rolla Anderson, who's run the tournament since 1957. "A lot more than there used to be. But I think both the parents and the players are better controlled than they used to be. It's become more professional, true, but there are also a lot more kids who are better."

Dr. Anderson, like Pat Jensen, knew junior tennis was still repairing its image, still cleaning up its act. The memories of the damage inflicted four years earlier were still fresh, the wounds still healing.

"That story made me so angry," Pat Jensen said bitterly. "If you go to any high school, and ask the kids where their parents are on a Friday night, most won't be able to tell you. But ask tennis players, and 80 percent will tell you their parents are with them, at the tennis club.

"When you get into this sport," Pat Jensen said, "you become such good friends with your kids."

Ah, *that* story.

In November 1982, *Sports Illustrated* told the rest of the sport public what the tennis world already knew too well: successful junior players were burning out, quitting the game, hurting themselves psychologically, and in at least one case, committing suicide.

Under the title, "The Glitter Has Gone," the magazine profiled Lori Kosten, a Memphis, Tennessee, teenager who'd dropped out of the game at sixteen despite a remarkable and precocious career. Kosten had won seven trophies before her eighth birthday and had been ranked as high as number two in the country in her age group. She'd beaten several players who'd gone on to turn professional, and newspapers had given her results considerable coverage, even publishing her admitted goal: to be the next Chris Evert.

Kosten was like many other successful juniors, the magazine suggested. Her parents had been deeply involved in her competition, and they had formed an apparel company—Little Miss Tennis—after Tracy Austin began wearing one of the dresses Marilyn Kosten, Lori's mother, had designed. Lori began to catch and eventually eclipse her older sister Julie, causing them a period of great strain. And Lori herself had come to view anything less than winning a tournament as failure. Stress and pressure began to affect her physically and psychologically, the magazine said. Eventually she quit.

"I felt like killing myself," Lori Kosten told *Sports Illustrated*.

There were other horror stories in the report. Howard Schoenfield, who'd won Kalamazoo in 1975 and joined the pro tour, suffered such an emotional trauma that he never touched a racquet for nine years. And the effects extended well beyond tennis. The pressures left him confused, disillusioned, and lost. Jake Warde, who'd grown up in Denver, Colorado, in the midsixties and who'd been compared to Australian great Rod Laver, walked off the court in a 16-and-under tournament and never returned. "One day I couldn't serve," he said. "The nerves, this time they wouldn't go away."

And there was the tragedy of Jennifer Amdur.

A close friend of Lori Kosten, Amdur had been ranked in the top 10 of her age group nationally, beginning with the 12-and-under division. Like Kosten, the story said, she was sensitive to the pressure of junior tennis. A few months after playing in the 1981 national Girls' 18-and-under Clay Court Championships, Amdur became anorexic. Her weight dropped dramatically, and she went under the care of a psychiatrist. Finally, alone in the family home one day while her father played on their backyard court, she stepped into a closet in her room with a shotgun and killed herself. Though her father told *Sports Illustrated* that he doubted the game directly contributed to her death, the implication the report made was clear: fast-track junior tennis can be tragically dangerous to a young player's health.

Statistics circulated at Kalamazoo in early August suggest that many children who take up the game now shy away from formal competition. According to one release, there are over 10 million junior tennis players in the United States, but only 86,000 boys are members of the United States Tennis Association, a prerequisite for playing sanctioned tournaments. The vast majority of the USTA's junior males don't compete, however; just 20,000 are active at the district level, where local junior tournaments are organized. The USTA, partly in response to these figures, has begun a variety of programs introducing the sport into public school systems and urban communities and teaching the basics of good sportsmanship and fair play.

"There's a growing division between children playing the sport for recreation, and those who are competing," says Dr. Ron Woods, the USTA's associate director of its Education and Recreation Center. "We're now trying to bring more attention to the young recreational players, who've been neglected."

Role models — that is, the lack of them — have contributed to the decline. At the height of the national tennis boom, in the early seventies, a Gallup poll estimated there were 20 million tennis players in the country. Polls today suggest the figure's dropped to 13 million. Fifteen years ago, the country's top players were sportsmen like Stan Smith and Arthur Ashe, and cool young teens like Chris Evert. Jimmy Connors was an angry young kid who, with maturity, would outgrow his outbursts. Billie Jean King was intense, but fair. The current top American man, John McEnroe, is a disruptive presence, and the system has been reluctant to curb his emotional outbursts. "It's not junior tennis that should be getting the black eye," argues Rolla Anderson. "It's the professionals, and it's not their fault. The players aren't being controlled [by tournament officials]."

The lack of control, the fact that tennis has plenty of inherent pressure in the play itself, the sheer expense of time, money, and emotion in developing a young player have made performing as a tennis parent one of the most difficult roles a mother and father can choose to play. Unlike baseball, where kids usually get their exposure to the sport through an organization like Little League, tennis's organized competitions for children can send shudders of fear through many parents.

"Junior tennis can be a vicious kind of life," says Ron Woods. "The serious players are finding too much pressure to compete for college scholarships and professional careers. Many of us close to the game are keeping our own children away."

Others find it irresistible. The examples of Aaron Krickstein, turning pro at 16 after reaching the quarterfinals of the United States Open, and Floridian Mary Joe Fernandez, in the Wimbledon quarters at 14, suggest how quickly a prodigy can make money. Krickstein and Arias earned substantial six-figure incomes in their first year alone. College scholarships, travel, media attention—all come to top junior players. And for parents like Pat Jensen, competitive tennis can become a way of life, an opportunity to structure a family around sport and competition.

"To say, like *Sports Illustrated* did, that tennis parents are pushing their kids to drugs is just not true," Pat Jensen concludes. "We're sacrificing a ton for them."

Murphy Jensen began struggling early in the second set of his third-round match against Californian Carl Chang. Riding the euphoria of his exhibition doubles victory the night before, where he and Parker surprised Aaron

Krickstein and Swedish pro Henrik Sundstrom, Murphy won the first set 6–4. But Chang, a stocky and several-inches-shorter baseliner, began to find his serve. Up 5–0 in the second, Chang listened incredulously as Murphy started to challenge his line calls.

Pat Jensen, sitting directly behind the baseline of Court Three, one of the eleven-court stadium's four "show" courts, turned to one of the handful of other tennis parents who'd joined her in a gesture of mutual support.

"It's amazing what the mind does," she said. "I did my job."

"You got him here, right?" said Jim Spencer, whose son was scheduled to play in an hour.

"Right," said Pat. "I got him breakfast."

Murphy continued to struggle, and early in the third set, Pat left to call North Carolina, where the twins were. Maybe the news was better there. "Where'd my mom go?" Murphy asked a few minutes after she left.

"Don't worry," Spencer assured him. "She'll be right back."

The news from the south wasn't much better. "They've been out there since ten A.M.," Pat reported. It was now past one in the afternoon. She noticed that Murphy had a dry T-shirt on. "At least he changed," she said.

Down 1–4, Murphy continued to complain about line calls. "You can't be grumbling, can't be tight," Pat said quietly. "You gotta play some good points." Loudly, she shouted, "Go to war!"

Murphy glowered in her direction.

"It's the only tournament on the whole circuit where you have more than sleeping parents," Pat shrugged. "The players aren't used to the talking."

At 1–5, Murphy found his game again, saving two match points and climbing back. Three games later, he was in striking distance, needing only to break Chang's serve again. But Chang held on for the upset. Pat Jensen wasn't displeased.

"Don't get me wrong," she said. "I love to win. But to do the best you can do, each day, that's all I ask."

There would be plenty of other opportunities to win, Pat figured. Murphy was going to Philadelphia, the girls to Ann Arbor, Luke to Cincinnati, then Murphy to Indianapolis, and all finally to New York City for what would be the last family reunion before Christmas. Yes, there'd be a lot more matches, a lot more chances.

But, Pat felt certain, what she'd given her children was considerably more than a win-loss record.

"The memories," Pat Jensen said, packing up to move to another court, to share the pressure with another parent at another child's match. "The memories are more valuable than the trophies, the gold balls, or the wins."

1 THE RISKS ARE REAL

For nearly two decades, coincident with the emergence of open professional tennis and a prize-money circuit that has awarded top players earnings of more than $1 million annually, more than a million preteen and teenage athletes have joined organized junior tennis programs in the United States.

In any given year, nearly 100,000 youngsters — some as young as seven years old, others on the verge of their nineteenth birthday, most between eleven and seventeen — compete in a network of tournaments at the local, regional, and national levels under the regulation of the United States Tennis Association and its subsidiaries. The locations of these tournaments range from New England to Alaska, Hawaii, and the Caribbean. Some young players are entering no more than one or two community events, perhaps an end-of-summer recreation-department championship. Others are playing what amounts to a 12-month circuit, spending tens of thousands of dollars to crisscross America, often traveling with an entourage that includes parent and private coach, and attracting the attention of international sporting goods manufacturers who, in turn, are lavishing them with thousands of dollars' worth of free equipment and clothing.

As disparate as their accomplishments and commitments are, these junior tennis players are sharing in the experience of a sport that puts unique demands on boys and girls. The competition, the stress, the sheer pressure of playing tournament tennis—whether the event is a block from one's home or thousands of miles away, whether in Kalamazoo, Michigan, or Miami, Florida—have few parallels in children's sport. Neither baseball, nor ice hockey, nor soccer—all of which have well-organized, comprehensive national junior programs beginning, in some cases, as early as six years old—ask as much of a young player. Although the stereotypical image of tennis as genteel exercise, as upper-class sport for the idle rich, still persists, such an image is misleading and false.

TENNIS'S UNIQUE PRESSURES

Tennis is tough, a solitary competition that forces the player to perform at his peak without coaching, without substitution, and under tremendous physical and psychological pressure from an opponent. And this is true whether the player is an adult or a child. In junior tennis, the player is alone. The problems to be solved are his, not a team's. The pressure is his, not his linemates'. Success, or failure, is his. There's no pitcher to chastise, no goalie to blame.

"As someone who has played in the juniors and as a professional," Chris Evert Lloyd wrote in *World Tennis* magazine, "I can say there was more pressure in the juniors." Junior players are, for the most part, immature physically and unsophisticated intellectually. Yet the game they're playing refuses to take the growing process into account. The points they're winning and losing are the same points Martina Navratilova and John McEnroe must conceive and execute.

The demands tennis places on a young player include effort, concentration, endurance, and the opponent. Once the match is under way, it must be completed. If a player has to take a break, that player's defaulted. If things aren't going well, if a stroke isn't working, the player still must continue. There's no opportunity to pull oneself together, to regroup, to take a break on the bench while the coach sends a substitute into the game. The player makes or breaks a match on his own, and everyone—opponents, officials, spectators—is aware of that.

The need to concentrate is underscored by the sport's prohibition on coaching except under unusual circumstances, such as international Davis Cup matches. A match may last three hours (at the 1986 Boys' National Championships, *first-round* matches were averaging nearly two hours), yet if the coach—who could be a father, mother, brother, sister, or tennis pro—suggests anything, no matter

how insignificant, the player could be penalized and ultimately defaulted. Even the exceptions — the brief rest period allowed between the second and third sets, if a match
goes that long, and high-school tennis, where neither
rankings nor trophies are on the line — can add, rather than
relieve, pressure. (A few states — Massachusetts, for one —
have taken cognizance of this and now permit coaching
and rest between each set.) Having just one opportunity to
glean advice on turning around a match hardly makes for
a relaxing moment. And even the correct advice can be
difficult to implement. United States Davis Cup captain
Tom Gorman's recommendation to Tim Mayotte that
he press forward with his serve-and-volley game against
Mexico's Leo Lavalle in the 1986 quarterfinal still left the
American facing two match points an hour later before a
screaming, hostile Mexico City crowd packed around the
slow, red clay court.

Fortunately for Mayotte, Gorman, and the United
States Tennis Association, there was no clock on the field,
and in the end, the match turned. Just as often, however,
the lack of a rigid time frame adds to the difficulty of the
sport. No lead, because there is no preset ending, is satis-
factory. Assuming that a two-, three-, or four-game lead is
sufficient can be disastrous, because an opponent can always come back, even when one point away from a 6–0,
6–0 defeat.

Many of these pressures — the need to concentrate, to
be fit, to sustain an effort — are true of other individual
sports. But unlike gymnastics or diving, tennis features a
real, physical opponent as well. Those sports that, like
tennis, involve fine motor skills — eye-hand coordination,

footwork, trained muscle response—don't throw in the fundamental additional problem of an opponent. How would a Dorothy Hamill or a Rosalynn Sumners react if, in a free-style skating competition, they were both on the ice at the same time, jockeying for the center space while trying to perform their spins?

Not, it's likely, with the same intensity a tennis player brings to the court. There, the complicated series of movements and shots is made *in combat.* "Go to war!" may be an exaggerated metaphor, but every shot a player makes is, in fact, in response to some strategic effort directed at him. There is no planned series of exercises, as in gymnastics. Everything is spontaneous. Everything a player does is an attempt to disrupt, deliberately, his opponent's rhythm of play. A tennis player is not only controlling his own play, he's trying to control the other's too.

The disruption can occasionally lead to cheating, and in tennis—which is usually played without third-party officials except at the pro level and certain top junior and amateur events—sportsmanship can, and invariably does, influence the outcome of every match. Unlike opponents in other sports, the tennis opponent can take a point that's rightfully the other player's simply by calling a shot that fell within the lines out. The point can be the most important of the match, and there's literally nothing the wronged player can do at that moment.

The simple pressure to win can turn players into cheaters, and that reality—whether or not it actually takes place—adds still more emotional pressure. Dr. Rolla Anderson, who for 29 years has run the national championships for 16- and 18-and-under boys' age groups, recalls a tournament official being called to a court by one player upset, the official figured, over a call. "When he got there," Dr. Anderson says, "he realized the match hadn't started.

" 'What do you need me for?' the official asked the boy who'd called for him.

" 'He cheated me on the racquet spin,' the boy complained.

" 'Well, even if that did happen,' said the astonished official, 'that hardly seems reason to get me down here.'

" 'Yeah,' said the boy. 'But it's the *second* time he's done it.' "

Because tennis is a fine-motor-skill sport, any kind of change can lead to serious disruption. In skating, a small imperfection in the ice can result in a fall that ruins an entire routine. In tennis, the opponent is constantly trying for major disruptions. In other sports, like football, bicycling, or running, disruptive emotions can be channeled positively against the opponent. That anger and frustration, whether it's from a missed holding call or a loose elbow to the ribs, can be vented immediately. But in tennis, that venting or release can disrupt a player's stroking and concentration. And that is exactly what the opponent hopes will happen.

When a player begins to make errors, they arrive in clusters. In golf, a top player—a touring pro on the Professional Golfers Association circuit—might make one mistake a hole and think he's played a terrible round. In tennis, on the other hand, one mistake every five or ten minutes—the time it takes to play a 400-yard golf hole—could be as close to perfection as a nationally ranked player can perform. In junior tennis, the mistake clusters occur more frequently than at the pro level. And each time a ball goes into the net, or over the baseline, the opponent's mother or father can clap and cheer. Mistakes become the object of instant ridicule.

The need to maintain equilibrium lets opponents apply emotional pressure by accusation. Being told you're a cheater, even when you're not, can throw off your game, particularly if the point is critical. "The pressures on world-class juniors are every bit as intense as the pressures on pros," Butch Buchholz, the executive director of the Association of Tennis Professionals, which represents the top touring male professionals, wrote in 1985 for *World Tennis*. "As a junior I treated every call as a life-or-death matter since I knew only one or two juniors turn pro each year."

Junior tennis is hierarchical, a pyramid that eliminates losers at every level, whether it's the top players or those first-year competitors moving out of novice events. A junior player becomes eligible to be ranked in his district after as few as three or four tournaments in a calendar year. The clear pecking order adds to the perceived risks and values, as well as to the player's self-esteem. With the time invested — two or three years' worth of lessons at the least — a player develops a sense of whether he should or shouldn't win in a given situation. Rankings and seedings add another layer of pressure.

The financial investment in a junior tennis player can add still more pressure on the court. A player doesn't become accomplished — can't even effectively play a set — just by picking up a racquet and hitting. At the highest levels of the game, stories abound of precocious genius: Evonne Goolagong and Jimmy Connors hitting balls at age two, Aaron Krickstein playing with his nationally ranked sisters at four, Chris Evert Lloyd and Tracy Austin serving at three. Yet all grew up, with the exception of Goolagong, in tennis families. Connors, Austin, and Lloyd had tennis pros as parents. Training came early. And none were born with backhands.

For a junior to learn the game, others *have* to be involved: parents, teaching professionals, perhaps — eventually — full-time coaches. Like gymnastics or skating, the practice time required costs a great deal, especially in regions where tennis can't be played outdoors 12 months a year. With court costs typically around $20 an hour at indoor clubs, and teaching pros charging anywhere from $25 to $50 an hour (more for an instructor with world-class pupils, like a Nick Bollettieri or a Robert Lansdorp), the expense of putting a junior player on a regular practice and training schedule is considerable. The junior player is aware of this. So are his parents.

Parents may not be aware of the other aspects, though. Many parents of junior tennis players haven't played the game itself, at least not at the level their sons or daughters are competing at. Perhaps they played when they were kids, too, at camp, or later as adults, in a regular social foursome or a round-robin climaxed with a potluck supper. They haven't been on the court in a tournament, in the midst of the sheer craziness of the event. An 11-year-old or a 12-year-old by himself against the world can be a very tough proposition.

Understanding the emotional pressures and the complexity of the sport itself is the first step for a tennis parent. "I don't understand what you're making such a fuss about," one father of a struggling junior told his daughter's coach. "What's so tough about playing? It's just a game. But in close matches, say the score will be 5–4 in the second set, my daughter will lose seven times out of ten. Why?"

"Do you play?" the coach asked him.

"Yeah," the father replied. "But not in tournaments."

"Fine," the coach said. "Here's what I want you to do. Contact your sectional association, and get a schedule of area B-level men's tournaments over the next couple of months. Map out a schedule for yourself over that period, trying to play five weeks in a row. And I want you to remember just one command: win. Go out and *win*! Nothing else matters."

A month and a half later, the father returned. Subdued and shaken, he told the coach that, for the first time, he understood what it meant to *have* to win.

"The impact of what you said was unbelievable," he said. "For the first time, I felt constant pressure on a tennis court."

REWARDS AND CASUALTIES

That the nature of the game is tough and demanding by no means diminishes its rewards. Nor should the inherent pressures chase children, and their parents, away from the sport. First and foremost, tennis is a life sport. If a child can handle tennis, first to master its strokes, then to use them in competition, he can handle virtually anything adult life has to throw at him. The key to getting the best out of the junior game is establishing the proper framework in which to take up the sport. Tennis can produce casualties — whether it's a Tracy Austin, whose preteen and teen successes in the professional upper echelons left her with a damaged back and retirement at 20, or a junior whose motivation to compete disappears. Given the nature of the sport, that's hardly surprising. Burnout isn't uncommon; the International Tennis Federation acknowledged its prevalence in 1986 by publishing a booklet on the subject. A handful of recent cases have even suggested that the stress of sanctioned match play can trigger, and has triggered, latent mental illness and, most extremely, suicidal tendencies.

But those are just that, the extremes. For the vast majority of young people — several million any given year — tennis is a teaching aid, preparing them for the stress and pressure of life. They learn about problem solving; they learn relaxation skills ranging from effective breathing techniques to discipline and concentration. When the child and his parents can keep the demands of the sport from exceeding the child's ability to cope, then there are few, if any, negatives about tennis.

"If I were a parent," Andrea Jaeger once told *World Tennis*, "and my kid was good at something, I'd encourage them. Not push the kid, but encourage. You should make them realize that they're good."

A young player who's having trouble with the sport and its pressure usually exhibits doubt, confusion, guilt, anger, resentment, then either temporary or complete loss of motivation and, finally, partial or terminal burnout. The on-court problems can travel off-court as well. Anorexia and bulimia are diseases female juniors share, and college women's team coaches say those physical problems carry into the early twenties as well.

Loss of self-esteem hits both sexes. Successful young players at all levels build identities around their games, tying their egos to wins and losses. One 11-year-old from Florida said, "As my tennis goes, so goes my life." When she missed qualifying for a national event, she was devastated. Stephen Anniston, a nationally ranked collegiate player at the start of the 1984 season, turned to drugs when he began to doubt himself.

"Tennis turns into life out there," Anniston told *World Tennis* magazine in 1985. "There's pressure each time you play. It's just you every day."

Anniston was the only child of a troubled family whose parents were divorced when he was 14. Through high school, he lived with other families, including his coach. As a sophomore at the University of California at Irvine, he played in the number-one singles position, and by the end of the year he was ranked sixteenth in the country. Then he broke his foot and had to stop playing. He turned to drugs, first for pain, then because he'd grown depressed over the lack of competition, the winning. "My foot took the athlete's world away," he said. He was arrested in a disco parking lot, charged with possession of cocaine, and enrolled in a rehabilitation program. After a brief comeback, he was dropped from the team and went into a hospital for an operation to correct his still-damaged foot.

"Tennis was my only foundation," Anniston concluded, reflecting on his short career. "When it failed, I felt suicidal."

In Anniston's case, and in the cases of other young players whose lives lack balance and careful parental support, the demands to succeed that tennis makes can result in the loss of the player's belief that he can do *anything* at all well. Juniors, even preteens, can feel like losers, like they've lost their sense of inner direction, their passion for what they do, even their passion for life.

When that happens, kids will rebel. They will lose their tempers. They'll do crazy things, struggling against the obsessive wall of pressure that tennis can build. They'll injure themselves to escape the sport. Like Stephen Anniston, they'll turn to drugs.

THE PARENTS GET HOOKED

Parents can get lost, too. Fathers and mothers may dream of their son or daughter turning professional. They may look at Carling Bassett, who turned pro at 15 and won nearly $60,000, or Aaron Krickstein, who beat Vitas Gerulaitis at the United States Open a few weeks after his 16th birthday, turned pro, rose to the top 10 in the world, and earned approximately a half-million dollars in prizes and endorsement fees before he was 18. They may anticipate fame, even glory, for themselves.

If those dreams come, however, they usually evolve slowly. At first, the parental involvement is innocent enough. The sport seems fun, the lessons are great for the youngster, and the costs—in both time and money—are minimal. Then those costs begin to escalate. Instead of local travel, the player has to start driving across the state — or into neighboring states — for tournaments. More practice is needed, and better practice partners. The child's talent emerges, and the parents are hooked.

In seeing the child develop as an athlete and competitor, a parent may transfer his unfulfilled athletic dreams and needs to the young player. That happens often, and inevitably the child is devastated. The parents must maintain a balance; projection can't be done in a healthy way. Take the Schneiders (not their real name). John and Mary Schneider's daughter, Kristen, had just turned 16 and earned a top-10 ranking in her age group. The family had been tight-knit when Kristen began playing, but the town they lived in was small, too small to provide the competition the Schneiders decided their daughter needed when she began to easily win every local tournament she entered. Nor were they delighted with the local pro. "This wasn't an environment where Kris could reach her potential," John Schneider tried to explain. But John's business kept him from moving, so Mary set up another residence in a nearby city, taking Kristen with her.

John Schneider wasn't worried. "Kris will be a fine player," he said confidently, "really fine." At the least, he figured, he'd save himself four years' tuition at a top university. The investment would be worth it. But soon it became apparent that it might not. With the second home, the more expensive lessons, and the travel to national tournaments, John discovered he'd spent $52,000 in Kristen's 17th year, as much as a bachelor's degree would cost. And what was worse, Kristen was growing apathetic toward the game, no longer eager to compete.

"I feel like I'm tearing up the family," Kristen finally admitted one afternoon after a desultory practice. "Mom and Dad are spending too much money, and it's because of me."

The guilt Kristen was feeling was putting too much additional pressure on her for her to enjoy the game. Yet John Schneider was oblivious. Kristen was just moody, he believed, just going through a stage.

"She's eager," he insisted. "She's fired up."

But his final comment revealed more.

"What do I do now?" he asked rhetorically. "After $52,000, do I just stop?"

Out of balance, the sport can become a nightmare, another failure experience for the entire family. "Our child has talent," parents will tell themselves, as they apply for a bank loan or remortgage their home. "This is our chance," they'll whisper to each other.

That's dangerous thinking. A young player may decide that he has to win, or else he'll become invisible. He may eventually need counseling. Mortgaging the present for the future can create severe emotional trauma for everyone concerned. There won't be any payoff at the end of the junior's career, only further payout.

The value in learning the game of tennis and playing it well has to be of the moment, in the present. "If today was the last day I ever played this game," a child ought to be able to say, "it was still worth it." And the best assessment a parent should be able to make on his son's or daughter's tennis is that the game was healthful, added to the child's self-esteem, and made the player more mature and better prepared for life.

That is the ideal balance for parent and junior to strike.

Yet that balance is so hard to strike. Tennis offers the illusion of early rewards, the impression that precocious talent will be rewarded with wealth and glory. That vision obscures the pyramidal structure of the system. There's less room at each successively higher level, and most touring pros — world-class athletes in the top 200 or 300 in the world — don't earn enough money to meet the expenses of a year's travel on the tour. Meanwhile, there are hundreds of other players struggling to qualify to join that same tour.

Few parents look this far ahead when their son or daughter first plays. They get involved instinctively, and producing a John McEnroe or a Steffi Graf, the West German prodigy who ranked third in the world at age 16, is the last thing on their minds. The mother or father will hit a few balls and eventually play a few games with the child, often at the end of the parents' own hour of play. Tennis is no different than a picnic or a round of miniature golf — just family fun. Then the parent decides the child has promise, a sense that's corroborated by the local pro. After a series of lessons, the child tells the parent he'd like to play a tournament. Mom and Dad agree, off they go, and their child's whipped. Neither Mom nor Dad is delighted with this turn of events, and they discuss how to avoid its happening again. There are more lessons, more practice. Either Mom or Dad begins spending more time on the court, not only feeding the child balls to hit but suggesting strategy, too. Apparently, the greater effort pays dividends. In the next tournament, the child wins a match.

With a victory, the excitement begins to build. Another tournament comes, and more wins, perhaps even a trophy. The parents and the child are happier still. Then there's a setback. The child loses to a player both he and his parents feel is less talented. "Come on," urges the parent on the drive home, "you can do better than that."

"I don't know," responds the child. "Maybe I should try a different sport."

"No, stick with tennis," urges the parent. "You've come too far to think about quitting now."

The child agrees, and he continues with his lessons and practice. When he's on the court, however, Mom and Dad begin to notice personality changes. Whereas the child once played calmly, he now will lose his temper, yelling at himself and his opponent. In a close match, the young player will call a ball out, even though his parents, watching from the sidelines, see it as clearly in. His opponent will argue, but to no avail. The match will continue.

"We'd better talk to him," Mom and Dad think. But they procrastinate. The game's become more complicated for them, too—the travel, the time, the expense—and although they're more sophisticated, the information they're taking in is still being processed. They're constantly having to deal with change, they're adjusting, they're stressed. Why shouldn't our son be given the same latitude? they think.

The scenario proceeds. More money is spent as the child advances to sectional, then regional play. The politics of the system begins to become an issue. Mom and Dad are concerned about the child's ranking information: has it been properly assembled and turned in? Did the regional officials play favorites and bypass the child? What about seeding? Mom and Dad have become a *lot* more sophisticated. What was recreation has become business, and the child's play is no longer child's play. Tennis is now an investment, and the dividends are wins.

"My parents never asked me if I won or lost when I came home from practice," Billie Jean King noted in her 1978 book, *Tennis Love*. "They just wanted to know if I had fun." Yet so many parents instinctively move in the other direction, rewarding their children for victories and punishing them for losses.

"If a parent runs up to a 12-year-old after she wins a match to congratulate her," says Harvard University tennis coach David Fish, "and if a tennis pro tells her after a victory that, with a bit of work, she could become *really* good, then that kid is being told she's more valuable than when she was just playing the game for fun and exercise. And, by extension, that she's less valuable when she doesn't win, and doesn't practice. That's when the real pressures start."

Other parents are less subtle. Privileges may be withheld, trips canceled. Even the promise of a better education may be held out as a carrot on a stick. The end result is the same. The child is taught that winning is the end. Mom and Dad have fundamentally altered their relationship with their son or daughter. And no one is fulfilled. What began as a healthy family pastime has evolved into something very unhealthy.

To avoid the damage, to cope with these risks, parents need to be trained. Like their children who play competitive tennis, they're performers. They may not step into the

Coliseum like their young gladiators, but they play as public a role as their prodigies, affecting not only their own players but everyone in the game their players interact with. Which is not to suggest the risks aren't worth taking.

"Being a parent myself," says Harvard coach Fish, "I know being a parent in general is a risk. If you're not a risktaker, you don't have kids. You don't have control over a lot of things. But if you can act as a partner in that growth, then they'll develop their own styles. And parents can be more effective partners than they realize."

It's a matter of training.

2 TRAINING PARENTS FOR COMPETITION

Hugh Rosenbaum could not tolerate failure, either on the tennis court or off.

The Rosenbaums (the family's name and certain other identifying characteristics have been changed to protect their anonymity) had reaped the rewards of this philosophy. In the decade and a half since the birth of Karen, his oldest daughter, Hugh Rosenbaum's driving work ethic had propelled his stock brokerage to the top of the financial-services heap in the Sun Belt city where he'd opened his office. His suburban home was large and spacious, and the backyard tennis court gleamed with a new DecoTurf II surface.

The ethic seemed to be paying off for Karen and her younger sister, Betsy, too. At fourteen, Karen had earned her first regional age-group ranking and now, two years later, was on the verge of national recognition. Betsy was progressing even faster.

Hugh Rosenbaum was deeply satisfied. Not a tennis player himself, not even an athlete (although he'd dabble at golf with his clients), he'd at first been amused by the game. But when his daughters began to show a talent for hitting balls—Karen had begun winning matches two years after her first lesson at age eight—he committed himself to an investment in their ability. First the private lessons. Then the court. Then the travel to the regional tournaments and, with luck, the national events.

"I want you to be the best you can be," Hugh told his daughters, and he encouraged them to practice through a system of incentives. Both Karen and Betsy had to sign on and off the court on a daily basis. Each had a minimum number of hours to put in per week, and both were expected to win on the weekends. If the results were acceptable, they would be given phone privileges, and Karen could use one of the family cars and stay out late on Saturday night, unless she had to play the next day.

For Karen, the incentives were subtler. When she won, the household was warm, caring, and attentive. When she lost, she got a cool reception—"the cold shoulder," she'd tell her friends at the private school she attended. Eventually the pressure took the joy of the game away from her. Karen didn't want to go to tournaments any more, because her father would be there watching. She decided she wanted to stop playing. Unfortunately, she couldn't bring herself to tell her father.

Hugh Rosenbaum was puzzled by the change he began to see in his oldest daughter. On the court, Karen had grown lackadaisical, almost disinterested. Her court logs were incomplete. In the morning, she had trouble getting out of bed. What was worst, Hugh thought to himself, she was losing to girls she should beat.

"Life's good if you're a winner," Hugh told her one day. "That's been my philosophy in business, and it's my responsibility as a parent to teach you what works for me.

"Failures," he warned Karen, "have it tough."

But Karen continued to flounder. Hugh agreed to his wife's suggestion to let Karen talk to a psychologist. But in Hugh's mind, the session proved fruitless: for the entire 45 minutes, Karen wept. *Wept?* What kind of a competitor, thought Hugh, was that?

Eventually, Ann Rosenbaum told her husband that, perhaps, it was time for Karen to quit. "I've made an investment in her," he responded. "She can't stop now. What's so tough about tennis? It's just a game. Look at Betsy. She can't get enough of it."

But Karen's depression continued. Furious, Hugh finally agreed, with conditions.

"If she wants to stop playing, fine," he said. "But she's got to understand what that means. There'll be no car, no allowance. She'll have to get a job. And, at the end of this school year she'll have to go into public school. That's the way life is."

By now, though, Karen's choice was easy. She stopped playing. Two years later, Betsy was ready to quit, too.

Hugh Rosenbaum couldn't understand this either.

REALIZING THE IDEAL PERFORMANCE STATE

As often as not, parents of young athletes do not understand how to help their children in competition. Perhaps they themselves are frustrated athletes, seeking a reflected glory long overdue. Perhaps they assume that what works in the boardroom works on the playing field. Perhaps they confuse parenting with coaching. Whatever the case, many parents will react instinctively to the pressures and stresses a young athlete experiences, and those impulsive reactions can make a difficult situation worse. Much worse.

"My father," Chris Evert Lloyd has said in *World Tennis*, "taught me one important lesson: to not be afraid to lose." When John Newcombe's father developed a pattern of criticizing his son after a loss, Newcombe told his mother that he'd refuse to step on the court if his father continued to accompany him to age-group tournaments. *Père* Newcombe got the message and became a supportive parent.

Feeling pressure to win and not being frightened about defeat are fundamentally different psychological states. Many parents misunderstand the latter, assuming that a drive to win, to succeed, means there will be less likelihood of a loss, and disappointment, for a child. Yet this is not the case. "You have to enjoy it, the thrill of winning," concedes Australian great Rod Laver, the current champion of the senior professional Grand Masters tour and twice winner of tennis's Grand Slam (the United States, French, Australian and Wimbledon singles titles). "You don't have to have the agony of defeat. [What you should be feeling is] just that you're disappointed, and you've learned something."

In the past decade, significant scientific evidence has been discovered indicating that the *absence* of pressure, rather than a get-fired-up-or-you're-doomed approach to critical points, is a characteristic of peak performances by athletes in all sports. This startling conclusion—most commentators, fans, and observers had assumed just the opposite—was first developed in 1978, after a series of interviews conducted by the Center for Athletic Excellence in Denver, Colorado, attempted to tie specific emotional climates to the outcome of events. Forty-three athletes in seven different sports—tennis, golf, swimming, basketball, football, track, and soccer—were asked to recall their best competitive performance and describe in writing what their internal psychological experience had been like during play. The same group was asked to repeat the exercise, focusing on their worst performance. The similarities in the descriptions were startling, regardless of whether the athlete played a sport like tennis, with its fine motor skills, or football, which emphasizes gross motor skills.

In the descriptions of personal bests, words like *energized, optimistic, effortless, automatic, alert,* and *self-confident* were repeated, even when the sample of athletes grew to several hundred. Phrases like *physically relaxed, mentally calm, low anxiety, mentally focused,* and *in control* were used over and over. No one claimed they had felt great pressure. All, on the other hand, suggested they had managed to avoid putting pressure on themselves when they were at the top of their game. It was as if, in achieving a particularly high level of concentration, they had put themselves in a near trance, a euphoric state that excluded external pressure.

That unique emotional climate was titled the Ideal Performance State, and in the ensuing five years, techniques were developed that would allow a player to achieve the state while in competition, rather than cross his fingers and pray that the tennis gods might smile on him that afternoon. Learning these techniques—visualizing winning strokes and points before they're played, relaxing muscles, projecting the image of a fighter and winner, controlling breathing—became Mental Toughness Training. Later in this book, we'll describe ways in which a parent, and a young player's coach, can work with a child in developing mental toughness.

With the success of players like Aaron Krickstein, Tim Mayotte, Todd Witsken, Susie Mascarin, Susan Sloane, and both Tim and Tom Gullikson, Mental Toughness Training and psychological preparation became an element of most topflight junior programs (not surprisingly, given the belief of Jimmy Connors—perhaps the most mentally tough player of the Open era—that the game, at his level, is "95 percent mental"). But the psychological research into what makes an athlete a champion, and what produces sporting excellence, has shed further light on the influences that lead to peak performance. One study, conducted by former English Olympic track star and United States college coach David Hemery and published in 1986 in Canada, surveyed 62 champions in 22 sports, ranging from golf's Arnold Palmer to baseball's Pete Rose. The Hemery study found that 98 percent of the world-class athletes came from homes described as "stable," and all athletes said their parents were consistent in their behavior. While 92 percent described their parents as supportive, 95 percent said those mothers and fathers did not "push" the athletes, as children, into competition. Few, in fact, specialized in one sport before their midteens. Of all the athletes, Chris Evert Lloyd, at age nine, was the earliest to begin specializing.

The Hemery findings reinforce research performed by two university professors at Vanderbilt University in 1985. That study, written by Dr. Gian Sihota of Vanderbilt and Dr. Choudi Sihota of Tennessee State University, used responses from questionnaires filled out by 200 top junior tennis players playing a championship in Nashville, Tennessee. They found that top juniors did not come from families whose parents were exceptional athletes, nor were the parents deeply involved in competitive sport. Access to facilities and, more importantly, a commitment on the part of one parent—usually the father—to spend considerable time hitting balls with the child while the basic strokes were being learned were dominant influences shared by those high achievers.

Take John McEnroe. He picked up the game at eight, and until ten practiced primarily with his father. His mother, Kay, has described herself in the book *McEnroe: A Rage For Perfection* as the "pusher" in the family, telling author Richard Evans, "I have never been one to accept second best." His father, on the other hand, played a more passive role during McEnroe's junior days. He took up the game when his son did but kept his primary focus on his career as a lawyer. He cheered his son's successes but did not pressure him to constantly rise to greater levels. Citing a 1959 study by psychologists Rosen and D'Andrade, Evans and Dr. Allen Fox, coach of the nationally ranked Pepperdine University men's tennis team, noted that among boys there is a great difference between high achievers and low achievers depending upon which parent pushes. "Nothing is more intimidating for a young boy than to be driven by a father who keeps demanding, 'Be like me!' " wrote Evans in his 1982 biography of McEnroe. "If he is forced to compete on that unequal level, his ego is in grave danger of being crushed. The same is not true as far as the mother is concerned. The boy is not trying to emulate his mother. He is merely trying to please her." John McEnroe's parents, concludes Evans, struck that delicate balance between constructive support and destructive pressure.

That balance, and how to find it, are the fundamental issues for the parents of a junior athlete. In searching out the solutions, parents should be questioning themselves and their motives. What do I do to help ensure that the sport experience is a positive life experience? How do I, as a parent, move that experience in the right direction? If my children never play this sport another day in their lives, will they be able to say it has been good?

In a pressure sport like tennis, parents can lose their perspective quickly. They can excuse unhappiness and stress, even financial sacrifice, for some hazy future goal — a national ranking, a college scholarship, a professional career. Both parent and child can be miserably unhappy, yet neither will admit it. So the parent has to constantly evaluate the rightness or wrongness of the child's competition: how is it affecting that developing person?

Parental instincts are often wrong, and the application of extraordinary pressure can have emotional consequences for the player like loss of self-esteem, loss of self-confidence, loss of motivation, and eventually, burnout. Yet parents rarely think of themselves as responsible for those negatives. They're more concerned about achievement goals and motives, the ones that quickly produce positive results in the win-loss column. The emotional effects are put on a back burner.

The consequences of parental pressure and instinctive, rather than trained, behavior can become physical, too. A child who is suffering injuries is often a child under great stress. Injuries can become a means of escaping the pressure, and the parent should monitor a child's physical condition. Is the junior player pushing too hard physically? Are the children eating properly? Are they rested? These are issues appropriate for the players' parents to involve themselves with.

WHAT PARENTS SHOULD BE DOING

"We were careful not to put too much pressure on," Jeanne Austin is quoted as having said, in *A Winning Combination*, by Julie Anthony and Nick Bollettieri. Her daughter, Tracy, won the United States Open championship as a precocious teen. At 20, she retired with a chronic back injury. "We never wanted her to feel she had to win to please us. Too many times, it's the parents who want their child to be a champion, and that doesn't work."

The Center for Athletic Excellence's research into the Ideal Performance State suggests that the Austin family's approach is precisely the one that *will* produce champions. When an athlete is experiencing his finest hour, he is likely to feel almost no stress, no anxiety, no pressure. The energy he's drawing is coming from a different source than fear or anger. The biochemistry at work is the result of positive emotions, and that "flow" state, as some psychologists have come to describe it, is powerful. The athlete is faster, quicker, and smarter, and he enjoys himself more. The emotional climate is pleasurable, and the state itself is obvious to the observer.

The parents' goal—and that of the player's coach or teaching pro—is to help the athlete get control over that energized state. Tight, tense situations in competition typically create the opposite climate. A player, feeling the tension, turns to his negative emotions for energy. Anger, perhaps temper, will emerge. Or the fear response will result in choking. In the most extreme circumstance, a player can become unmotivated, afraid of putting himself on the line. Take Milan Srejber's performance in the 1986 United States Open. In his victory over American Todd Witsken, the six-foot eight-inch Czechoslovakian performed a series of rituals before each serve, methodically pacing to the baseline, taking a full 30 seconds before each point (Witsken complained, to no avail, that the delays were even longer), then quickly rushing the net to hit winning volleys. In the following match, when Srejber faced third-seeded Boris Becker, both the performance and the results were a stark contrast. Srejber took no time whatsoever between serves and abandoned his ritual pacing behind the baseline. He halfheartedly approached the net and often didn't bother to even wave his racquet at Becker's returns. Becker won easily in straight sets (6–0 in the third) in a match that had been expected to be close. The change in Srejber's game was so radical that commentators Mary Carillo and Barry MacKay—both matches were televised nationally—assumed Srejber was ill. In the press conference later, however, Srejber said no, he felt fine. Perhaps a bit nervous, he added, but fine.

Srejber had tanked, which is not to say he'd thrown the match. Unable to handle the stress and the thought of losing, he became incapable of giving a 100-percent effort. He withdrew emotionally from the match and abandoned the competition.

Tanking occurs at every level of the game and offers no less a challenge for parents of junior players than it does for coaches of world-class competitors. Parents should strive to get their children to develop a challenge response to these pressures. Players can be taught to get fired up in an emotional way so that they *want* to compete, so that they want the challenge the opponent represents. When they have such an attitude, the match is something exciting for them. The junior player is able, when he's learned this response, to maintain the flow of energy from his positive emotions and to play consistently at the upper level of his ability. For parents, the task is to find ways to make that happen on a consistent basis, and to ensure that the demands of the situation don't exceed the skills and the talents of the player.

How can a parent help the child experience the Ideal Performance State? Just as the player himself does, by achieving a delicate emotional balance. The parent must build the player's confidence, reduce external pressure, increase enjoyment, and stimulate self-motivation. He must help the child to become a positive thinker, to be in control and alert, and to develop a sense of relaxation and calm during play.

This is not to suggest that the parent become coach. Most of the significant research done on peak performance and the Ideal Performance State evolves from the late Dr. Abraham Maslow's theories on human motivation. The father of humanistic psychology, Dr. Maslow, at the time a professor at Brandeis University in Waltham, Massachusetts, pioneered research in excellence, choosing high achievers as subjects of his inquiries. From these studies, Dr. Maslow developed a theory of behavior based on a hierarchy of need motives: that is, for a human to realize his potential, he has to fulfill certain needs.

Dr. Maslow ranked the needs on five tiers, the most basic being those that perpetuate the human race: an air supply, food, water, sleep, and sex. Humans obtain those through procreation, nurturing, and tending, Dr. Maslow observed. At the second level are safety and security. Families of achievers, reasoned Dr. Maslow, provide fulfillment on both tiers. The third level consists of love and a sense of belonging, which can be provided—in the case of top athletes—not only by a family, but by a coach or team or all three. The needs for self-esteem and the esteem of others come next, and these needs can be met by the rewards found in sports, or by parents. The highest level—self-actualization, where someone becomes what he's capable of being—corresponds to the Ideal Performance

State. Until the lesser needs are met, a young athlete can't reach level five, and meeting those needs, for the child, is more important than wins and losses, rankings and trophies. If there is deficient love, or little sense of belonging, or insecurity, or lack of self-esteem, then achieving as much as possible on the playing field is out of the question. And the more parents get into coaching, the more likely they'll be ineffectual in stimulating the emotional climate and in fulfilling the needs of their children at home. Coaching should be left to coaches.

Choosing the right coach, on the other hand, is the parents' responsibility. But as the child improves, the parents have to back off from coaching the player's physical skills and from getting too involved with winning and losing. As Tracy Austin told Nick Bollettieri and Dr. Julie Anthony in their book, *A Winning Combination*, "My parents did such a good job. They knew exactly how much to push and how much not to push. I don't really like to say push, because you might interpret it in the wrong way. They just pushed me a little bit in the beginning. Sometimes I'd be lazy and want to go play in the sandbox, but my parents would have me hit balls. Or I wanted to stay out late during a tournament and my parents wouldn't let me.

"Some mothers drive me bananas," added Austin, "because I see them pushing their kids so hard. They hit their kids balls, keep them on the court for hours and scream and yell at them. The kids are crying and you know they hate tennis. As soon as these kids can quit tennis, you know they're going to quit."

Parents should concentrate on the child's emotional development and provide the opportunity for the child to find success on the tennis court. And what is success? Ponder these statistics: of the 100,000 regionally competitive junior tennis players in the United States, only 1,200 will receive national rankings. No more than 10 juniors in any given year — and, on the average, far fewer — will turn professional. And fewer than half of those will ever break into the top 100 players worldwide, the level at which a player *might* make a living at the game. A parent should understand that the chance of his child becoming a star is remote, next to zero.

ARE YOU A PROBLEM PARENT?

How do parents become problems? How do they violate their attempts to help their children toward success? There are 10 characteristics of a parent who's hurting, rather than helping, his son or daughter the athlete.

Problem parents create additional pressure outside that of tennis itself. Tennis is a game in which pressure is a constant dynamic. Any undue emphasis on winning exacerbates that already-present stress, which is more than enough for any young athlete to handle.

Problem parents resort to the use of fear. These parents use punishment and the withdrawal of love to get their children to perform better. Unfortunately, it works . . . for awhile. Their kids can get very good, and the criterion of improvement suggests to the parents their technique is correct. The children improve, and they develop substantial skills. But the attendant emotional risk proves dangerous to the children's health and well-being over time.

Problem parents criticize. These parents lose their objectivity, getting caught up in the ethic of winning and losing. They have no distance from their son or daughter. They lose perspective on the experience and are of no value as people who can help massage the emotions and get the child back into some kind of sane arena.

Problem parents rarely understand expressions of insecurity. Research underscores that kids who express high-anxiety traits often have parents who are insensitive to the indications of those traits. The children will say that they're afraid to play, or nervous, or feel under tremendous pressure. "It's not that big a deal," these parents will say.

Problem parents show negative emotion. A pacing parent on the sidelines, agonizing over close calls, puts even more pressure on a young player.

Problem parents think negatively. Negative thinking is a poor model for juniors, and indeed, negative thinkers are not what the parents want their children to become. Nor do these parents see the incongruity between what they're asking their children to do and what they're doing themselves.

Problem parents nag. They are constantly on the children's backs, suggesting that they haven't been training properly, that they aren't doing enough jump-roping, that they haven't been paying attention to their match scheduling. These parents feel they've been doing their job—underwriting the expenses and providing the transportation—and their children haven't been holding up their end of the bargain.

Problem parents foster guilt. Guilt is used to get the child to perform the way the parents desire. "I've done so much for you" is a typical remark. "The family's made so many sacrifices. The least you could do is take more advantage of this great opportunity we're giving you." The child is made to feel that the rest of the family isn't vacationing, isn't saving, and doesn't have free time because of his tennis.

When the child loses, he's thinking, "Everyone's doing so much, and I can't do my part." At its extreme, the child can feel accountable for husbands and wives separating into two households so that the young player can train in a more favorable part of the country. That kind of relocation is not, in and of itself, a mistake. But managing such a move without guilt is a delicate balance indeed.

Problem parents make tennis bigger than life. A match, a tournament, is blown out of proportion. Everything else in the family takes a back seat. If a youngster's self-esteem is tied to winning or losing, this overemphasis can have tragic results. A child shouldn't feel less valuable when he loses. Or less loved.

Problem parents overlook critical areas of development. If a child's doing well in tennis, problem parents will allow him to get away with murder in other areas of his life. A kid can be permitted to treat people badly, with little respect. One well-known high-school coach, Bob Wood of University Liggett School in Grosse Pointe, Michigan, says his junior players are so socially immature that he spends the first practice of each season lecturing them on proper manners. "It takes 10 minutes," Woods says, "just to teach them how to look someone in the eye when they're shaking hands." The lack of self-discipline hurts the young athlete who, when competitive tennis comes to an end, must compete in the classroom and the workplace.

Even success on the tennis court cannot guarantee a maturity off-court. The glamour, the stroking of a young star can give him a false sense of the world.

For a parent to succeed in tennis, he must look beyond the outcome on the court. If the goal is to have the child become the best player he can be, then the reality means standing back, taking pressure off, and nurturing and supporting.

The junior tennis player's ultimate ambition is to play in his Ideal Performance State. To do that, he must be mentally tough.

And his parents have to perform with that same mental toughness.

3 LEARNING TO BE MENTALLY TOUGH – AND TO KEEP THE PRESSURE OFF

THE PLAYERS

David Smith learned how treacherous the game of tennis can be. So did Marco Cacopardo.

A Colorado teenager, Smith had risen to the top of his age-group rankings in the Intermountain section and had convinced his family to send him to a southern tennis academy, where he could hone his game against players better than he could find around Denver. Smith had surprised himself, holding his own and better against the top juniors in the country. The word traveled west, and when David Smith returned home, he was seeded second in the sectional championships—even though, as a 13-year-old, he was playing in the 14-and-under division as one of the youngest entrants.

Although his ground strokes were ready for the challenge, his mind wasn't. The altitude bothered him, and he felt he suffered a bit from jet lag. In his worst nightmares, he imagined — after his successes in Florida — that he'd lose in the first round in Denver. And when his opponent stayed close in the first set, that's what happened. Smith froze, and lost in straight sets.

Both he and his father, a former college player who'd coached his son, were shocked. But they had lost perspective. For David Smith, the first year of the 14s was unimportant in the long run. Wins here would not affect his future — they wouldn't determine what college he went to, whether he'd play professional tennis, or whether he'd get more or less free racquets and equipment. Eventually, David Smith returned to Florida and began rebuilding his game.

For Marco Cacopardo, the stakes were higher.

One of the country's top juniors in 1986, Cacopardo held a high national ranking in the 16-and-under age group. In midsummer, he was invited to the Junior Davis Cup tryouts. The Junior Davis Cup team is a group of eight junior players culled from the ranks of the 16- and 18-and-under divisions by the United States Tennis Association and given special training, clothing, and privileges. The latter includes wild-card entries into the draws of major professional tournaments during the summer, giving the amateurs an opportunity to play against the best players in the world without having to endure the rigors and pressure of qualifying. For a teen with any aspirations whatsoever of turning professional, a place on the Junior Davis Cup team is a major step toward reaching that goal. Cacopardo took his tennis seriously, and he understood the chance.

Playing well, Cacopardo looked as though he might make the team. If he beat Martin Blackman, a talented and athletic kid from New York City who reminded some of Arthur Ashe, he would likely be picked. And as the match progressed, Cacopardo's chances improved. At 5–2 in the third set, he served for match at 40–15. Then he became so nervous he could barely move. Muscles tight, heart racing, his body responded to the chemistry of fear.

Cacopardo lost the game, and the match.

The teenager's next tournament was the national hardcourts, where he was seeded sixth. There the pressure hit early, and he lost in the first round in straight sets. As in the Junior Davis Cup tryouts, he felt frozen.

"I couldn't hold onto my racquet," he recalled. "I couldn't move my feet. I felt paralyzed and lost. I couldn't even call balls out. I would open my mouth and nothing would come out. I was so scared I couldn't believe it. I felt like totally quitting the game. I honestly believed I couldn't play the game any more. My future was over."

Cacopardo's parents wondered what they should do as they watched their son floundering. "We had never seen anything like that before," Sheila Cacopardo said. "We felt helpless and very concerned." Eventually, they agreed to their son's request to drop out of the consolation round and return home to Forest Hills, New York.

Cacopardo's self-esteem was suffering, and he was confused. "I no longer felt the same about myself or the game," he said. "It was like I lost my ability to play, and I no longer saw playing as fun." Fortunately, his parents were sensitive to loss of confidence. They listened, accepted, and never judged as their son talked about his pain and fear. Although they didn't understand what was happening, they gave Marco the freedom to follow his feelings.

"Marco's feelings were first and foremost, and tennis was clearly secondary," said his mother. "We told him that whatever he wanted to do was okay. If he never played again, it would be okay with us; we just wanted him to be healthy and happy."

Two weeks later, Marco Cacopardo was back on the court. Reaching the quarterfinals of the Boys' National Championships at Kalamazoo, Cacopardo regained his confidence and his game. "I just decided to go out and do my best and have fun," he said. "If I lost in the first round, it would have been okay, as long as I gave it my best shot."

Channeling Energy

Because the Cacopardo family was able to keep the pressure off Marco, he could discover a new perspective on his game and begin to work toward the kind of internal emotional climate that would resist fear and anxiety. What had been high negative energy could now become high positive energy.

High positive energy? High negative energy? What does this have to do with parenting? Or helping a son or daughter in competition?

Plenty.

First, parents of junior tennis players, and of any young athlete, need to know that the quality of a child's athletic performance reflects the player's internal emotional climate, and that that climate depends upon the energy the player is drawing on for his feelings. How can feelings be so important in sport? Look no further than the 1980 United States ice hockey team that won the Olympic gold medal. In upset after upset, the Americans beat athletes that were stronger and more highly skilled.

"You're born to be hockey players, you're meant to be here," coach Herb Brooks told his team before they stepped on the ice to play the heavily favored Russians. "The moment is yours." The skaters that beat the Soviets that day were highly motivated and intensely positive. Nothing else could have given them victory.

At any given moment in competition (and in practice and any preparation leading to competition), a player is in one of four energy states: high positive, high negative, low positive, and low negative (see diagram, below). In one high energy state a player is angry, even raging. Flushed, tense, breathing rapidly and shallowly, the player is hostile and focused on the object of his anger, and on little else. Because, in the Center for Athletic Excellence interviews, the athletes rarely characterized this state as enjoyable, this high energy was termed negative.

Another high energy state reflected top performance. Players are relaxed, breathing deeply, with a strong though not pounding pulse rate. The mind is focused on the competition, yet simultaneously aware of the surroundings. Athletes said they loved to find themselves in this state, and it was termed positive.

51

	High	
High Positive Energy		High Negative Energy
Good Concentration Success		Poor Concentration Tunnel Vision Attention becomes too narrow
Pleasant ———————	A|B C|D	——————— Unpleasant
Poor Concentration Easily distracted Attention becomes too broad		Poor Concentration Mixture of High Negative and Low Positive
Low Positive Energy		Low Negative Energy
	Low	

Two low energy states were defined in the research, too. One, where the muscles were relaxed and the mind was calm, though unfocused, was determined to be pleasant, and positive. Even so, it wasn't conducive to good performance. Players in this state were easily distracted and couldn't concentrate on their play. The other low state revealed even more inconsistency and unpredictability.

Not only was little muscle tension evident (leading to poor reactions, strength, and stamina), but the athletes were also suffering from tunnel vision and had poor concentration. In the first low energy state, the athletes were relaxed; in the second, they most definitely were not.

Bringing high energy to a competition, and managing to stay relaxed while using that energy, are the keys to top performance. While a player's game is described as intense, it's really simply energetic. Intensity is high energy, and in its most positive state, intensity is closely linked to feelings of aggression and determination. When parents and coaches of young athletes look for intensity on the court, they're seeking nothing more than the high positive energy state.

Not one of the athletes interviewed by the Center for Athletic Excellence found their Ideal Performance States evolving from any other kind of energy. Relaxed and energized, they could enjoy their play and execute without tension, regardless of which of the seven sports they played. Yet parents, particularly those who've not competed at high levels of sport, assume that winning athletes perform their best *under* pressure.

Not true.

In the course of researching and establishing the Ideal Performance State, it became clear that athletes who perform particularly well under pressure are *not*, in fact, under pressure. In their minds, they've eliminated the sense of anxiety and tension the spectator assumes. To do that, these athletes have disciplined themselves to think positively about the *challenge* that competition poses—not the threat.

The Results of Negative Energy

Reacting to competition, and its inherent stress, as a threat triggers a biochemical reaction in the body that evolved in primitive man: neurotransmitters in the central nervous system and hormones in the blood combine to pull blood from the digestive system and the fine muscles in order to energize the body's big muscles. This was useful if the person under stress was being challenged by, say, a mastodon or saber-toothed tiger; today, it's helpful if you have to lift a Volkswagen off your next-door neighbor or mother-in-law. But if the stress stimulant is Martina Navratilova's net game, or Mats Wilander's backhand, or reasonable facsimiles, then being able to run as fast as one can to the nearest cave or wield a small tree trunk like a club is not the precise capacity called for. There's plenty of energy, but not a great deal of control.

With a pounding heart, with adrenaline pumping, the athlete is poised for flight. On the court, however, there's no place to go. To serve an ace in a third-set tiebreaker, one needs calmness, relaxation, and positive energy. Once the biologic alarm has been triggered, that internal performance climate is impossible to maintain.

When a junior doesn't respond to competition, an internal state resulting from low negative energy occurs. Likewise, when a young player reacts by developing high negative energy, one of two other internal states emerge. These three states are tanking, temper, and choking. And it's important for parents to be able to recognize them and understand their root causes.

Tanking. Tennis players tank when they give up attempting to win points and playing competitively. At every level of the game — even among world-class professionals — tanking occurs, most often when one player decides that the other is superior, and that nothing the inferior player can do will make any difference in the outcome of the match. At the 1986 United States Open, Ivan Lendl made a remarkable run across the court to retrieve a drop shot off the racquet of France's Henri Leconte and return the ball for a winner — even as Leconte thrust his arms in the air in celebration of what he assumed was his own winner. "I won two sets with that shot," Lendl said later, noting that Leconte had been ahead 5–4 when he hit what he'd thought to be unreturnable, and that the Frenchman proceeded to lose – with little effort – nine of the next ten games.

Players often believe they can protect their self-esteem by tanking. In not giving an effort, they can tell themselves that they weren't really beaten. Yet, by the same token, they guarantee their failure. In the Center for Athletic Excellence's research, shifting into the low energy state – whether it's positive or negative – never produces a peak performance. In deadening the emotional reaction to a loss, a player can no longer draw upon the energy required for the Ideal Performance State. Externally, it may appear to a coach or parent that the player no longer cares. That's almost never the case. The player cares too much. And, not surprisingly, criticizing the player for what appears to be an ambivalent or apathetic attitude can result in an angry, defiant response.

The key to avoiding tanking is commitment. If a player can keep himself committed to the competition, he won't withdraw. Willing himself to enjoy the situation, to be challenged by it, to tell himself that he loves being the underdog, that he wants to fight, is the kind of thinking that can tap into the necessary positive energy. Parents and coaches, who are sometimes the only spectators watching a young player's match, can contribute to the moment with positive support and encouragement. Parents can tank, too, and walk away from a losing effort. They've got to remember that they're also performers. Even if they don't like their child's emotional state in play, they've got to keep an even keel.

Temper.   Netting a volley on game point or mishitting an overhead can cause a player to berate herself. A questionable line call can lead a player to believe that everyone involved in the match—her opponent, the umpire, even the tournament officials—is against her.

Amy Schwartz believed the world was out to get her. One of the country's top juniors in 1985—she won the Easter Bowl 16-and-under division, made the finals of the national Girls' Clay Court Championships, and earned a national ranking—Schwartz had to overcome a temper that was virtually uncontrollable. "I can't stand to lose," she would explain. "Maybe I want to win too badly. As soon as it looks like I might lose, I start to boil inside."

Like John McEnroe, Schwartz used her temper as a way of firing herself up. Without her rage, she found it difficult to generate any high energy. "I'd start choking and playing real tentatively. Eventually I would start getting mad again and start playing better. But it never lasted. I never play great when I get angry," she told us.

Amy Schwartz's temper caught the attention not only of her friends, family, and coaches, but of tournament officials as well. Unlike McEnroe—whose marquee value led officials and tournament directors to tacitly condone his behavior up to a point (his tirades did get him uninvited from playing Davis Cup tennis)—Schwartz was warned that her behavior was unacceptable. She began to struggle to change. Both her parents and her coach agreed to work together toward this goal. First they had a match of hers videotaped. Schwartz admitted to them that she was shocked when she saw herself lose control. Next she was encouraged by her coach to measure a match's success not in terms of winning and losing, but rather of playing her best for as long as she could. Finally, she was asked to rehearse, in her mind, how to handle crises like questionable calls or bad luck. Project a powerful, positive, and calm image at all times, she was told. Slowly, Amy Schwartz grew more composed on the tennis court. "I've learned that if I don't constantly work on it, my old habits are right there to defeat me again," she concluded.

Unlike someone who tanks, a player like Amy Schwartz who reacts to stress with temper is energized. But that energy is characterized by nervousness, fear, anxiety, frustration, and a desire for vengeance. None of these moods allows for concentration or relaxation. Parents shouldn't condone short fuses in their children, even if that means stopping their play. An enforced vacation from the court won't damage a budding champion's prospects for success. Bjorn Borg developed a reputation as one of his country's notorious hotheads. Finally, after an angry and embarrassing outburst, Borg's coach, Lennart Bergelin, took his racquets and locked them in a closet. For three months, the superstar-to-be wasn't allowed to play. When he returned to the game, he was a changed personality. The Ice Man was born.

Parents who lose their temper are giving implicit permission to their sons or daughters to do the same. The pressure, the stress has to be accepted, not rejected in a fit of anger.

Choking. How bad a rap does the verb *choke* have in world-class sport? Aaron Krickstein found out in 1984, his first year on the men's professional circuit. Playing in Chestnut Hill, Massachusetts, at the United States Professional Tennis Championships, Krickstein won a surprisingly close first-round match against a Brazilian qualifier, veteran Joao Soares, coming from behind in the third set for the victory. At a press conference after the match, Krickstein, just 16 at the time, confessed he was never concerned about losing.

"Soares has a reputation for choking," the Grosse Pointe, Michigan, teen told the assembled press. "He does it all the time."

The reporters nearly swooned in disbelief. A pro athlete accusing another of *choking*? Unheard of. Pros treated one another with kid gloves, knowing it was enough to take an opponent's money. Leave the pride and self-esteem alone, the unwritten code said.

Krickstein's father, Herbert, a Detroit pathologist often traveled the circuit with his son. "Please don't use that," Dr. Krickstein asked the sportswriters. "Aaron's young. He's still learning."

Choking, to a junior who's had considerable competition and whose parents are trained to understand mental toughness, is hardly the epithet that pros (and those who follow professional sport) consider it. Aaron Krickstein himself probably knew that, even if he was the only person in the press conference with that knowledge. When a player chokes, Krickstein understood, he is still trying. He has neither given up nor lost his temper and his concentration. Top junior coaches—Nick Bollettieri for one—will not chastise players for choking. Those players are too close to performing well.

What is choking? Simply fear, fear that the player can't achieve what he set out for himself as a goal. Like temper, it's the result of a high negative energy state. Real, physical symptoms are that the heartbeat is too fast, the muscles too tight; the fine motor skills controlling the player's stroking and footwork are not operating the way they should. Unlike the temper state, there is no rage. The anger is turned inward—to sadness, despair, and frustration.

Self-control stops the choke. The more emotional control a player can exert, the less frequent the choking, and the briefer the choking episodes. Parents have to understand that criticism of choking—which every young athlete in the world is guilty of at one time or another—can turn a player to either temper or tanking as an alternative. And both those states guarantee mediocrity. Far better a player thrust himself into the challenges that lead to choking.

When a child is choking, he's still competing. He's fighting, caring, taking the risk. The commitment's there, and the parent, when the match is over, ought to be applauding.

THE PARENTS

Do's for the Trained Parent

As we noted, the goal for the trained parent ought to be to help the child perform under the best possible emotional climate. The parent should stimulate ideal performance conditions, helping their son or daughter to relax and achieve calmness. Parents should reduce external pressures, and those internally induced, and should emphasize that the sport's fun and enjoyable. The parents' positive attitude will give the child personal confidence, and that confidence will give the emotional controls that help young athletes take an abnormal path when problems come their way, see situations as challenges rather than threats, and avoid temper outbursts, tanking, and choking.

These are the true goals the parent of a young athlete should have. Winning means much less.

How does the trained parent achieve these?

Trained parents are focused on sport mastery rather than sport competence. Sport mastery is a phrase sport psychologists use in describing athletes whose focus is performance, whereas a focus on winning or losing is termed sport competence. University of Illinois psychologist Dr. Glyn Roberts, in a paper titled "Perception of Stress" (published in 1986), posited that overemphasis on sport competence and underemphasis on mastery accounts for the astonishing dropout rate of adolescents from competitive sport in America. According to Dr. Roberts's figures, 80 percent of all children between the ages of 12 and 18 abandon competitive sport. "The dropouts," writes Dr. Roberts, "are likely to be competence oriented." This certainly seems to be the case with junior tennis.

In emphasizing mastery, parents help the junior to be the best he can be. They should convince their child to risk giving a 100-percent effort, and to have the attitude that what will be will be. These parents understand that the child's emotional well-being, his development as a person, supersede everything else. Especially the outcome of a match.

Trained parents decrease the pressure to win. The parent emphasizes sportsmanship, ethics, personal development, responsibility, and attitude toward others. Trained parents model the behavior they want to foster. They're careful not to get caught up in the race to be number one, in the winning-at-all-costs ethic that comes on very seductively and subtly. Most parents will deny they've embraced it, but upon examination, they find they've got that orientation.

Trained parents have the perspective that tennis has value only as a preparation for life. The probability of one's son or daughter achieving fame or glory in the sport is, as we've noted, virtually nonexistent. The sport should be embraced for the qualities it gives its participants: problem-solving skills, positive-thinking skills, a work ethic, and self-discipline.

Trained parents understand the risks. The sport, as we've described, has real risks. Parents have to read the signs of stress—sleeplessness, the player's turning hypercritical, cheating, indications that the on-court personality doesn't reflect what they want their child to become. Juniors can grow irresponsible, ignoring the rights of others and treating their own property shabbily. Their egos can extend beyond what's healthy.

Tennis should be a healthy emotional experience for both parent and child. Self-esteem should never be on the line in winning or losing. The parents should instead emphasize sportsmanship and integrity. Parents who emphasize winning will be unable to hide their disappointment with a loss. "Why didn't you push harder here?" they'll demand to know when the child comes off the court. "Why didn't you come to net when your volley was working? Why didn't you question that call?"

A player can't go to parents who ask these questions. Nor, for that matter, can he go to coaches who do the same. And when that perspective, that balance is lost, both coaches and parents become ineffectual.

Trained parents ensure the coach is keeping the right perspective. The coach should be positive, encouraging, success-oriented. Parents ought to meet on a regular basis—perhaps once a month—with their junior's coach. The meetings should not criticize teaching methods but should discuss shared goals and emotional development. In New York City, the Stadium Tennis Club brings a psychologist in once a month to meet with both the parents and juniors in a large group setting.

Trained parents rarely step out of the parental role and into the coaching role. Parents may hit with their player, go to matches with him, and share some of the planning, but a trained parent doesn't get overly involved. Instead, he seeks out people who'll do the coaching and the training. The trained parent, in turn, builds a support system that makes playing and improving possible. These parents provide the funds and the wheels, the time and the shoulder to lean on before and after the match. That support is not tied to winning, nor are any family privileges.

At a tournament, parents will find themselves in a strange place with nothing to do. Their natural instinct is to throw themselves emotionally into the match. Trained parents don't. They'll watch the match, but they'll detach themselves from it by charting their child's winning and losing strokes, creating a tool for the coach to use at the next practice session. Ideally, their chart will include not only shotmaking but the match's emotional events, too— whether the child is tanking, choking, showing temper, or looking nervous, or whether he's exhibiting mental toughness by responding to the pressure positively. A parent caught up in cheering won't be an effective charter.

Trained parents don't show negative emotion. Unless, that is, it's a reaction to unsportsmanlike behavior. Parents who are trained maintain an equilibrium. They don't consider the money and time spent on junior tennis as an investment on which they have to get a return. They don't confuse their own needs for recognition with their child's. Those needs— marriages that have gone sour, faded athletic dreams, midlife crises—are a strong inducement to overinvolvement. Trained parents keep them separate. They know that tennis is not a team sport, that "we" don't compete.

Trained parents don't videotape lessons or take notes. Just as they don't coach, nor should they kibitz. They're not standing in the wings, trying to force motivation. Trained parents understand that overinvolvement can result in their child playing the sport for them, and that once they back off, the child quits. That possibility frightens some parents, yet when it occurs, clearly the intrinsic motivation is lacking.

Trained parents don't get lost in the pressure, the craziness, the pettiness. The parents of a good junior player are constantly wrestling with questions. Should our child stay in school or go to a tennis academy? Should he aim for college or try to turn pro? Should we move south to get a better tennis environment or stay where we are? Should one of us go to live with our child, the player, and the other stay to raise the rest of the brood? Are our dreams realistic?

Each question puts pressure on the family, and parents who are trained learn to perform themselves. They don't become embroiled in bitter arguments over which course to take. Nor do they avoid the issue by refusing to make a decision or take a stand.

Being a good tennis parent is a formidable task. No one should expect to find his way through the maze of junior tennis easily.

What to Look for in Your Child

If a trained tennis parent's role is that of supportive observer when a match is going on, what, then, should the parent be looking for on-court? Are there aspects of the child's performance that should be encouraged? Discouraged?

A tennis player can develop mental toughness in a number of different areas, research has shown. Any parent familiar with these can look for their evidence during a match. The areas are eye control, ritual, pace, breathing, intensity, image as a competitor, relaxation, managing mistakes, negative self-talk, enjoyment, and positive attitude. Obviously the areas are interconnected and dependent on one another. Yet deficiencies in one or some can clue a turn for the worse in a player's game, hinting at a choke, outburst of temper, or tanking to come. And proficiencies can be building blocks on which to remodel performance in the other areas. Underlying all is the philosophy that the mentally tough player isn't afraid to lose. This attitude is described as the challenge response, and it is the optimal way for a player to handle stress and pressure on the court. The professional tennis player with the greatest challenge response of the Open era is probably Jimmy Connors. As longtime rival Dick Stockton said of Connors in *Tennis* magazine, "If you're ahead of him, there are no free points. The guy just doesn't give up."

When looking for the challenge response in their son or daughter, tennis parents can focus on the following.

Eye control.   Maintaining a narrow visual field is important in holding one's concentration on the moment at hand. A player who is losing focus on the game is a player who's becoming distracted, perhaps nervous, perhaps disinterested. Whatever the case, the lack of eye control indicates a shift from the high positive energy state to something else, and the chances of performing well diminish. Mentally tough players will discipline themselves to keep their eyes on a specific object between points—the strings of their racquet, the baseline, the ball.

Ritual.   A ritual can be as simple as the number of times a player bounces a ball before he serves, or a complicated sequence of pacing, toweling, and adjusting clothing. Baseball players are notorious for the rituals they perform before stepping into the batter's box. The series of hitches, tucks, taps, and swivels is as carefully choreographed as a modern dance. Why should players ritualize? A mentally tough player — Connors for example — will visualize a point before it's played, seeing in his mind's eye the stroke, sensing the feel of a good hit. Performing a ritual before beginning a point gives the opportunity for visualization and slows the player down, setting a comfortable pace. Connors on important points will, in fact, lengthen his rituals, taking more time before a serve, and before the service return.

Pace.   Maintaining high positive energy through a match is impossible if a player is rushing. When points are beginning before the player's had time to think through what he wants to accomplish, he's given control of the pace of the match to his opponent. Impatience can indicate, too, that the player is growing nervous or angry. There's not much a tennis parent can do about that once a match begins, except maintain a sense of calm.

Breathing.   Certain breathing patterns contribute to emotional control. A player can pace himself, and lengthen his stroke, if he learns to exhale on contact. In practice, players might contrast their strokes by first holding their breath when they hit, then releasing it. Saying "yes" when the ball meets the strings can act as a trigger to the exhalation.

Parents can tell when their child is under stress by observing breathing patterns both between and during points. Short, irregular, jerky breathing signals stress.

Intensity. A player who is responding to the pressure by embracing it, by saying "I love it!" to himself, will generate the kind of positive energy that fuels top performance. Balancing the right level of intensity, we've noted, is enhanced when the energy is drawn from the positive emotions. Energy stemming from negative emotions such as anger or fear quickly leads to states of overarousal. Learning to read and adjust one's level of intensity (energy, excitement, arousal) is fundamental to competitive success.

Image as a competitor. Players can create the impression that they are fighters, that they are tough, by the way they carry their head and shoulders. Martina Navratilova is a good example. In the finals of the United States Open, playing Steffi Graf, Navratilova faced four match points. Each time, on the verge of defeat, she pulled her shoulders back, swaggered to the baseline, held her head high, and effectively cloaked the anxiety she had to be feeling. She never gave Graf the opportunity to think that, mentally, Steffi had weakened her. Parents can look for that kind of image projection from their children. Even calling the lines—whether the junior barks "out" loudly or softly— can suggest whether the player's a confident fighter, or something else.

Relaxation. Players who exert emotional control and respond to pressure understand the importance of being able to relax on the court. And their parents should be able to see them doing that. One simple method is to contract and then shake out the hand holding the racquet. This loosens the muscles in the wrist and forearm and helps the circulation through the arm and hand. Learning how to relax one's muscles, to read and adjust tension levels, is fundamental to being a good competitor. Relaxation on court can be enhanced by carrying the racquet in the non-dominant hand, by relaxing the shoulders, by stretching, and by following a precise ritual just prior to starting each point. There are a variety of muscle relaxation techniques that can be used off the court to aid a young player in this area: massage, music, meditation, and progressive relaxation training (a system of contracting and relaxing each separate muscle group).

Managing mistakes. Every player—even one who looks like a fighter, is relaxed, and is playing with intensity—will make mistakes. There are no perfect games in tennis. Junior players have to learn to manage their mistakes, and parents should be watching for these management skills. Expression, concentration, and emotional control contribute to that management. When a player mishits a ball, or hits it to the wrong place, he should simply turn away from the net and walk back to the baseline. Exclaiming "Oh no!", even slamming the racquet onto the netcord or waving it furiously through the air, only helps the opponent. Instead of demonstrating frustration, the player should try to tame the lion inside. Parents should encourage their children to look the same, whether the point was won or lost, whether the play was good or bad. If bad, the player should visualize the correction in his mind and keep his thoughts to himself.

Negative self-talk. The image to be projected is strong and silent. Corrections are to be made internally. Screaming at oneself, therefore, doesn't help the junior player. The less the player says, the better. If something has to be said, it should be positive, upbeat. For the parent, of course, the same holds true.

Enjoyment. A mentally tough player reminds himself that tennis is a game, and that he's having fun playing the game. If a parent sees the child in misery on the court, something's wrong. And if the junior is expressing unhappiness, he's hurting his game.

Positive attitude. Combining the sense of enjoyment with the desire to compete, to want to play well and—if it comes—to win, defines the positive attitude. The trained parent can't look inside a child's head, but he should always be aware of what the child is feeling about the sport and about competition.

4 THE PROPER PARENTAL ROLE:
STARTING OUT

Hana Mandlikova began playing tennis when she was eight, using a wooden paddle her father, Vilem Mandlik, gave her. There was never any pressure to succeed, Mandlikova recalls, because her father understood that sport should be fun. He was an ex-Olympic sprinter, the Czechoslovakian national champion. If Hana took to tennis and had any success, the pressure would come to her. The beginning was a time for enjoyment.

"For us, tennis was a family outing," Mandlikova says. "When I began to play in tournaments, both parents would come along. That was true for the other Czech juniors, too."

THE AMERICAN JUNIOR PRESSURE COOKER

Hana's peers in the United States weren't so fortunate. While virtually all relied on their parents to support their play, few felt the languorous atmosphere of a family picnic when they ventured into the tournament arena. For them, the philosophical fundamental behind competition was the late professional football coach Vince Lombardi's exhortation, "Winning isn't everything, it's the only thing." Lori Kosten, the focus of *Sports Illustrated's* scathing look at junior tennis in 1982, saw that axiom on the kitchen wall every morning; it was only when her burnout symptoms became too obvious to ignore that her father decided to take the plaque down.

And yet—although a generation of American parents embraced the Green Bay Packers' credo as gospel—Lombardi himself renounced it before he died. In an interview with sportswriter Jerry Izenberg, Lombardi said, "I wish to hell I'd never said the damned thing. I meant the effort . . . I meant having a goal . . . I sure as hell didn't mean for people to crush human values and morality."

Howard Schoenfield was nearly crushed.

The greatest player of his junior era, Schoenfield won virtually every match he played in 1975, including the junior titles at both Kalamazoo and Forest Hills. A year later, he'd dropped out of tennis. In 1986, he returned as a junior coach, scarred by the competition, but wiser for it.

"The pressure in junior tennis is unmeasurable," Schoenfield says. "The academies contribute. So does the

71

money. So do the people around the sport. The kids on the court these days are looking at the dollars at the end of the tunnel.

"In 1975, there was absolutely no relief for me. People were making a living off me and my tennis. The expectations were high, and I heard them everywhere I turned. I'd walk into a tournament, and everyone would expect me to win. I was *supposed* to win. All the time. And no one was there to tell me, 'Hitting the ball isn't the most important thing in your life. You're the same person, on or off the court.'

"My trouble was that I didn't have an escape mechanism, no way to blow off steam. You need someone who can move you away from the game, who can give you some perspective. This is a silly little game. When it comes to life and death, this is pretty stupid . . . no, insignificant. How you feel about yourself is what's important. Tennis, competitive tennis that is, undermines that if the parents aren't there to be supportive.

"My dad didn't understand that, although you can hardly blame him. He was, and most parents are, just as new to the experience as the players. It's tough sitting, watching a match. At least a player can vent his anxiety through play. The parent can't.

"Parents who think they don't have any problems down the road, those are the ones who better watch out. There are scars everywhere you turn around. There are people who never pick up a racquet again. Nine years it took me to get back on track.

"Now that I'm coaching, it's scary too, because I find myself doing a lot of the same things that were done to me.

But it's hard to let go, or back off. The tennis is my kid's, not mine. The coach can apply as much pressure as any problem parent. But he has to be both the good guy and the bad guy. He can be a friend, but has to hold the reins too. Yet he can't choke the junior. The years the junior plays tennis are years the child can't get back. Ever.

"I just wish someone with this insight had been around for me. Because this game's devastating. Absolutely devastating."

IN THE BEGINNING

Eight years old? Or seven? Or five? Or three? None of the above? When does it make sense to begin a child in tennis?

There's not a true consensus here. Some pros suggest the earlier the better, often citing the examples of Tracy Austin and Jimmy Connors, who were preschoolers when they first began hitting balls. Vic Braden, the outgoing, ebullient teaching pro turned sport psychologist who runs his eponymous college in southern California, is one. In *Teaching Tennis to Children the Vic Braden Way*, Braden recommends starting the child as young as three years old, and not waiting until eight or nine. At younger ages, Braden argues, kids concentrate on the ball better. The developing eye-hand coordination will help them with other sports, he says, and early exposure won't necessarily lead to burnout. "Kids don't get turned off by sport," says Braden, "but by overzealous parents."

And yet Braden, one of seven kids from a poor family in Monroe, Michigan, took up tennis late. When he was caught stealing tennis balls from the public courts near his home, his apprehender offered a choice: learn to hit a forehand, or go to the police station. Braden opted for a racquet, and two years later he was playing in state junior tournaments.

"And not once," Braden would remember years later in an interview with the authors, "did my mother come across the street to watch me play."

In that regard, Braden was an exception. For most junior players, parental involvement is more important than the age they step onto a court.

Psychologists considering tennis as competition rather than uncompetitive exercise suggest that competitive tennis is irrelevant before age eight, and of little benefit before age twelve. One study, conducted by the University of Illinois at Urbana, found that the mean age for starting tennis as a child was fourteen, although eleven was more typical. This study did not, however, differentiate between competitive players and those who were learning the game on a casual basis. (Interestingly, the study compared participation figures from 1977 and 1984, which suggest the sport may be on the verge of another boom: in 1977, 880,000 boys and 950,000 girls played; seven years later, the totals had risen to 1,350,000 and 1,240,000 respectively.)

"Not until age five or six do children spontaneously compare their performance with that of other children in order to evaluate competence," notes University of Washington psychologist Michael Passer. At that age, Passer says, kids just want to know who's best. Wondering how to achieve that success comes much later, not until ten at the earliest, and more commonly at twelve or thirteen. "To assess one's competence on outcome, on wins and losses, means the ability to figure out causal factors," Passer notes. "Strategy? Opponent's ability? How tough was it? Knowing history is important too. It's not until the ages ten to twelve that children look at the past to figure out the future. Not until then do they develop realistic performance expectancies and goals." Not until then, in other words, do kids begin to see competition the way their parents do.

Still, putting a child on the court to exercise has positive immediate benefits — it's a healthy thing to do for both parent and child. It also follows the pattern of behavior that the research available suggests is characteristic of the development of the sport's best players — a parent working with the child to instill a love of the game. More often than not, it's the father. David Hemery's research indicates that over 92 percent of the champions interviewed described their parents as "consistent," "supportive and encouraging," and "not pushing." Fifty-three percent said their parents had "no expectations" for competitive success, and another 27 percent said the expectations were "for education only," to use the prowess to win a scholarship. Eighty-eight percent had one or both parents familiar with the sport they played, but few had exceptional financial resources. Only 3 percent came from income brackets above middle class.

Tossing a ball to a youngster, encouraging him to practice off a backboard or a wall, or simply being willing to spend the time on the court can be enough for a parent to start a top competitor's career in tennis. Rather than spending the money for a lesson the child might not want, or have the physical maturity to handle, the parent can tailor each court session to his child's attention span and ability. With luck, he'll open a line of communication that will stay open through the later years, when parents often lose touch with their adolescents. The philosophy, if there need be one at all in these early years, ought to be "have fun!" "The bottom line for children in sports," said Fred Engh, president of the National Youth Sports Coaches Association, "particularly those under twelve years old — is that it's a learning experience, but above all it should be fun."

IS THIS THE WAY IT'S DONE ELSEWHERE?

No country that we're aware of has developed a better system for bringing children into the game than through their parents. There are, however, countries who've been fortunate enough to build either strong role models or noncompetitive philosophies on a near societywide basis. There are also countries — primarily socialist — that manage to remove the financial obstacles most American families face when struggling with the demands of topflight junior tennis.

Sweden's system has been a model for much of Europe since the midseventies, when Bjorn Borg emerged as the greatest player of his generation. Borg's on-court demeanor — controlled, withdrawn, emotionally stable — was imitated by most boys taking up the sport. The best of them were well-served. First Mats Wilander, Anders Jarryd, and Joakim Nystrom appeared in the world's top

25. By 1986, Stefan Edberg and Mikael Pernfors had joined them. (The women lagged behind—not surprisingly, given the five-to-one ratio of boys to girls in the Swedish junior programs.)

Because Sweden is small—its population of 8.5 million is approximately that of greater New York City—the national tennis federation can keep tabs on its players, and it has had some success in providing uniformity for introducing beginners to the sport. Youngsters in group lessons are started with undersized racquets and balls much like Nerf balls. They graduate to a "starter" ball, which resembles a regular tennis ball in appearance but isn't as lively and is therefore easier to control. Certain coaches—employed by the federation rather than by private clubs—are assigned specifically to beginner groups. The beginners are encouraged to rally on foreshortened courts—a net is strung across the length, rather than the width, of a court to get more players involved—before they're taught the proper strokes. And the costs are minuscule. A Swedish junior pays five dollars for his club membership. The message the federation sends to these beginners is simple: first and foremost, this is a *game*.

The encouragement is obviously paying dividends. In 1986, a reported 52,000 juniors were playing at the country's 900 clubs, about half the number reported by the United States Tennis Association to be participating here. If Sweden's population were comparable to ours, its junior tennis community would be in the neighborhood of 1.5 *million*. And who knows how many top-20 players?

Numbers, of course, don't guarantee competitive success. Japan is in the midst of an unprecedented tennis boom. According to the Japan Tennis Association, one out of every ten Japanese plays tennis, and there are currently 3,000 clubs in the Far East nation. The public courts are so crowded, the *New York Times* reported, that lotteries are held to allocate court time. Competition, however, is not part of the boom. The lack of facilities has compelled teaching pros to accent rallying and cooperation. And the role models—the country's best players—have had little or no success in the outside tennis world. In the spring of 1986, Japan's highest-ranked male was listed as number 428 on the Association of Tennis Professionals worldwide computer rankings. The best woman was no better. Winning, in other words, is not a means to becoming respected in Japan.

"A student may be aggressive," one tennis school manager told the *Times*, "but aggressiveness does not mean he can be a good tennis player. [Our philosophy] is not to be like John McEnroe. That would disturb the harmony of the group. Since this is a pleasure everybody is supposed to be enjoying without breaking the harmony. There are sometimes 20 students to a court, so everybody has to be in harmony. In case somebody stands out, that student is removed from the class and put in the more advanced class."

With one court for every 60 players, such a philosophy is, well, harmonic.

Role models who handle pressure well, and a society that provides the resources to allow a junior to play the game, open tennis up to children in a way this country has yet to do. When parents don't have to make their own financial sacrifices—sacrifices that turn tennis into a family

Yugoslavia's Monika Seles: the world's best 12-year-old was taught tennis by her father, who learned the game from a book.

Martina Navratilova: a study in concentration and strength, Navratilova's court presence radiates confidence, and her physique reinforces the impression of toughness.

Jimmy Connors: perhaps the most mentally tough player of his era. Connors combines a passion for the game with his will to win, love, and discipline that were developed early on, under the tutelage of his mother.

A young Hana Mandlikova: developed in the Czech national system of subsidized coaching and league play, Mandlikova was brought into the game by her father. "For us," she says, "tennis was a family outing."

John McEnroe: like many young players, McEnroe was brought to a coach, Tony Palafox, for evaluation. McEnroe's father — a bit anxious — wondered if his boy had any promise.

*Touring pro Terry Phelps, in the world's top
25: no pressure as a junior. "My parents,"
she says, "had other lives besides tennis."*

Coach Nick Bollettieri: he looks for three
basic elements in a young player. "The
desire to win," he says, "attitude, and—most
importantly—footwork."

Jimmy Arias: professional as a teen, coming back in his 20s. A player with, as coach Nick Bollettieri describes it, the "heart of a streetfighter."

*Aaron Krickstein: at 16, became the young-
est male ever to win a professional Grand
Prix tournament. When he began playing
the circuit, his father accompanied him.*

Luke Jensen: the eldest of the Jensen brothers, Luke became the world's top-ranked junior. His parents always intended him to be an athlete, they simply happened to get the sport wrong. "We thought he was going to play quarterback for Notre Dame," says mother, Pat.

*Murphy Jensen: when his football-playing
father began coaching high school tennis,
the Ludington, Michigan, players would run
road races to determine who played which
position in a match. "The memories are
more valuable than the trophies," says his
mother.*

Martina Navratilova with her coach of two and a half years, Mike Estep. For top professionals, managing the relationship between player and coach is no simpler than it is for the tennis parent.

The Estep/Navratilova partnership was the most successful in tennis, yet it ended abruptly in the winter of 1986, when Estep, bored, decided he wanted younger players to build into champions.

Marco Cacopardo: this top junior felt the pressure in an extreme way. At the national hardcourts, he "couldn't hold onto my racquet." "I felt paralyzed," he says, "and lost."

*Touring pro Susan Sloane and teaching pro
Fritz Nau. When Nau discovered the
Kentucky teenager, neither he nor she had
been playing for a full year. Twelve months
later, she was a state champion.*

Chris Evert Lloyd: "My father taught me one important lesson," she says, "to not be afraid to lose."

What it's all about: not the unreal dreams of professional success, not big-bucks endorsement contracts, just the satisfaction of playing the game well and being the best you can be.

business rather than a family pastime — they find it easier to look at the game as a game.

PARENTAL READINESS

Parents, too, have to ask themselves if they're ready to begin tennis with their children. Among the questions are, can I let my child get involved without becoming overly protective? Can I avoid getting overly involved in an unhealthy way? With young children, particularly those first feeling their way into competition, there's a tendency on the part of parents not to let go. Parents have to have the right philosophy clearly in mind.

First, parents have to realize their self-esteem isn't on the line. Parents often take losses harder than kids. Virtually every junior who's played in sectional or national competition has a horror story to tell — a parent furious about an unexpected loss, striking his child as he came off the court. A parent who cares more than the child does about winning or losing has already lost. The child will be fooling around with friends or playing in the school yard an hour after a match ends. The parent will still be fretting.

Second, the personal development of the youngster should supersede all other considerations and objectives. The parental overview should focus on the person, not the athlete. One recent psychological study noted that parents of gifted athletes rarely acknowledged their child's interests or talents in other areas, say, music. The same, in reverse, held true for parents of gifted young musicians. Parents who cannot see their child's whole life will not be prepared to create the kind of emotional climate he needs to succeed in tennis. The sport should be teaching the child autonomy—self-direction, self-control—rather than undermining confidence and causing personal turmoil and excessive stress. Tennis parents should understand that perspective—*before* they become involved.

Third, parents have to ask themselves, is the sport experience good for us? Or is it costing us emotionally? If the latter's the case, they've got the wrong philosophical attitude. They haven't prepared themselves adequately for the competitive world of junior tennis.

Parents have to keep in mind the risks and the danger signals. They can't get overinvolved and emotionally caught up.

THE TEACHING PROS' ADVICE: KEEP IT SIMPLE

America's top teaching pros—coaches such as Nick Bollettieri, Dennis Van der Meer, and Vic Braden—are unanimous in their approach to young beginners. The simpler the introduction to the game, they say, the more satisfying the experience will be.

"From ages four to eight," says Van der Meer, "we operate what we call the munchkins program. It's not really teaching, just doing all kinds of silly things. For an hour twice a week, we'll have the kids come onto the court with their racquets and play games. We'll tell them to 'make a sandwich,' where one rolls a ball on his outstretched racquet. That's an open-faced sandwich. Then another kid will put his racquet on top of the ball. That's a close-faced sandwich. Another ball on *that* racquet, and it's a Dagwood. Then another racquet, and it's a triple-decker. You keep on until the pile collapses.

"We try to keep everything competitive, even ring-around-the-rosy with a bouncing ball in the middle. Sometimes the parents will say they don't like this method, that their children aren't learning the proper grips, but I disagree. You're developing ball skill and ball sense. Then, at nine or ten—after they've learned some discipline and organization through the games—you can begin formal instruction."

Bollettieri emphasizes that coordination and agility are more important than hitting the ball when children are starting out. "For little kids," he suggests, "playing catch, gently tossing balls—even rolling them on the ground for them to swing at, letting them bounce the balls on their own racquets are good ways to begin." Don't worry about grips, Bollettieri adds, or the number of bounces a child lets the ball take before swinging. When the lessons begin, he says, they should focus on concentration, the proper ready position, and coordination between the feet, the hands, the eyes, and the racquet.

Like Van der Meer and Vic Braden, Bollettieri thinks it's pointless to delay introducing competition. "In tennis," he says, "it's impossible to avoid . . . but keep your expectations to a minimum. Let your child learn to enjoy the game."

"The beginner who moves too quickly," notes Braden in his book, *Teaching Children Tennis the Vic Braden Way*, "will have the urge to win and [so will] go for what's comfortable." That, however, will often be incorrect in way of technique. "Within 10 hits," he warns, "a child is already beginning to pick up bad habits."

Dennis Van der Meer feels, in the final analysis, that the concept of simplicity is difficult for American parents to embrace. "In Sweden, which is big on miniature tennis, using only a part of the court is much further along," Van der Meer says. "In the States, it's difficult to introduce simple techniques. American kids are so sophisticated. They want to look like Daddy. Their parents say, 'I want my kid to play like McEnroe. Why can't he stand facing the back fence when he serves?' "

McEnroe spent 10 years learning the game. Parents have to learn patience. Even genius takes time to emerge.

5 DEVELOPING THE GAME

It's not easy to convince parents to step aside and let their junior players develop their own games.

Twelve-year-old Michele Benson (not her real name) *seemed* to be coming along nicely. Her strokes were solid, and she was maturing as a competitor. Michele had broken into the top 10 in her age group in Florida, and into the top 20 in the 12-and-under division nationally. Her mother, Anna, was convinced she had a budding champion, a potential professional. And Anna Benson was determined that no one would stand in the way of that goal, even Michele herself.

Michele's mother oversaw every aspect of her daughter's tennis, from scheduling practices to choosing and entering tournaments. When Michele was on the court,

Anna Benson would be nearby, taking notes. She'd hired the coach, she figured. Why shouldn't she be monitoring his methods?

Like many juniors, Michele spent several hours on the court daily. Indeed, Anna Benson was convinced that her daughter's success in competition was in direct proportion to the amount of time she spent hitting balls.

Eventually, Anna Benson enrolled her daughter at the Nick Bollettieri Tennis Academy in Bradenton, Florida. Michele worked in a small group of topflight players and would play in bitterly fought intramural tournaments every week. She did well, it seemed to the Bollettieri staff. But not well enough, it turned out, for her mother.

One afternoon, Michele arrived at her appointed hour looking pale and weak.

"I don't feel well," she told her coach. "I have a sore throat." The coach suggested that the academy nurse examine her. The nurse suspected that Michele had a case of strep throat and recommended that her mother take her to a doctor for a throat culture. Anna Benson agreed.

After the appointment with the physician the following morning, Anna brought Michele back to the academy for her afternoon session. Michele's coach asked her how she felt.

"Not too good," Michele said.

"Maybe you should skip today," offered the coach.

"No," interjected Anna. "Michele hasn't been getting in enough tennis. She *needs* to play."

The following day, the test results came in, confirming Michele's strep condition. That afternoon, she arrived to play a match.

"What are you doing here?" demanded her coach. "You ought to be in bed. You were terrible yesterday. You're not going to be any better today."

"Mom wants me to play," Michele said quietly, and she took the court.

The coach found Anna Benson and confronted her.

"What are you doing to her?" she demanded. "This is crazy!"

"No," responded Anna Benson. "The question is, what are you doing? Michele's been playing terribly. She's not working hard enough. There's no reason she shouldn't play this match. She hasn't been doing well, and you know it. She needs to work harder, and this is a good place to start."

The coach fumed. Michele played, and lost badly. But not, ultimately, as much as her mother lost.

DEVELOPING PLAY

Just as there's no set formula for starting a young player in tennis, nor is there a surefire program for developing that player into a competitor. Between the ages of six and sixteen, children mature physically at different rates. They don't all grasp with identical swiftness the intellectual complexities of playing games. For every precocious player, every Tracy Austin or Andrea Jaeger, there are those who had unheralded junior careers, yet made fine professionals. Bud Schultz, who broke into the top 50 in the world on the men's tour, was an NCAA Division Three college basketball player at tiny Bates College in Maine.

Tim and Tom Gullikson, the identical twins from Wisconsin who were all-state high-school basketball players, went to a college—Northern Illinois University—where the tennis team was supervised by the football coach, and where there were no on-campus indoor courts. "When it was time to practice," remembered Rosemary Gullikson, Tim's wife, "the coach used to say, 'Get your mallets.' "

Neither Gullikson played a national junior tournament. Their best junior competition came from each other; they would routinely face off in the final of the men's division of the Wisconsin Open. Not until both had passed their twenty-third birthdays did the Gulliksons venture into professional tennis. By the beginning of the eighties, and until Tim's retirement in 1986, they were one of the United States' best doubles combinations.

"Their parents had the attitude that they should be happy playing sports," Rosemary Gullikson said, "and they never pushed Gully. But if he ever misbehaved, or threw his racquet, his mother warned him what she'd do. 'I'll go out on the court, take you by the hand, and stop you from playing right then,' she told him. 'You wouldn't,' he said. 'Yes I would,' she warned. And Gully never tested her."

To a certain extent, the healthiest way for a young tennis player to develop is belatedly. The pressures are fewer, and the child—who is by then likely no longer a child—is better able to cope. For one thing, the late bloomer often has the opportunity to compete in other sports at a fairly high level. Mike Estep, for two-and-a-half years Martina Navratilova's coach, was one of the first Americans to join the pro circuit at the dawn of the Open era in 1968. Four years before that, he'd been playing high-school football in Texas.

"There was no professional tennis at the time," Estep recalled at his home in Dallas, Texas. "I'd been playing in the national age groups since I was 14, but my goals were to get a college education and, if possible, to see the world. The money was no motivation. There wasn't any when I was in high school, and when I got out of college it was microscopic on the pro tour. Of course, once I started traveling, the money began doubling every year. But not at the beginning."

The summer Estep turned 16, he was ranked number two in the country in his age group. He'd won the Orange Bowl tournament in Miami, Florida, and had done well in the other major junior events, despite his rather small stature. (Five feet eight inches tall, he would later be nicknamed The Tiny Texas Tornado by tennis columnist Bud Collins.) But like most young Texans, Estep wanted to star on the gridiron.

"When I was a junior, I began practicing placekicking," Estep said. "I was determined to play senior year, and figured that placekicker was my best opportunity, being a midget. I went out to tryouts, and found out I was the fastest guy on the team. I wound up running back kickoffs, playing safety, and catching passes as the slotback."

It's a precedent that would make the agents, equipment representatives, and college coaches who hang around the national junior events today shudder with distaste. For Estep, though, it worked. He broke into the top 100 internationally in singles, did better than that in doubles, and managed to support himself as a player.

"You've got to keep in mind that the money on the tour does not relate to the abilities of a player," he cautioned. "The money, for all that's out there, is not that good. In my better years as a player, after expenses, I'd clear $25,000. And that's after the *tour's* expenses. I still had to pay for my house, my car, whatever. In 1980, when I was running a tennis club in Houston, I had assistants working for me who made almost as much teaching clinics as I had on the tour. A good ranking at the world-class level doesn't ensure money, unless you're in the top 30. If you show up with a hangnail, you can lose your match, and be in the red for a week."

The money, in Estep's view, has placed too much emphasis on success. And that, in turn, has led to a number of cases of arrested development. Because Mike Estep spends so much time around the women's game these days, he sees that trend especially prevalent there.

"The kids who do well early," Estep said, "stay with the same style. They're frightened to develop their games. The women build their games between ages 12 and 15, the men between 15 and 18 for the most part because they mature later, and need more of an all-court game to succeed. The women are still young, obviously, at 15, and they've learned to hit from the baseline. Then they turn professional, and they *still* hit from the baseline. They've thrust themselves into a stressful, pressurized situation, but they haven't finished developing. I think that's why the Czechs are so successful right now. They're not sending their country's top juniors out on the world circuit at 14 or 15. [Czech juniors are] working under a federation-subsidized national circuit, with its own coaches, until they're 21, and then they're given the option of whether they want to travel or not."

Estep's analysis raises another point: establishing a ratio of success to failure. As a parent works with and observes the child developing as a player, he recognizes that the youngster needs to feel a sense of achievement. Goal-setting in a practice situation can achieve some of that. Competition is limited to minigames. Small rewards for hitting a certain number of balls without a miss, or for hitting a certain sequence of shots, become reachable goals for youngsters still mastering the fundamentals. So can the first tournament experiences be, if they're carefully chosen. But a parent has to be alert to overexposing the emerging youngster to competition. Losing love and love the first time out may not be traumatic if the child has been around tournaments. But if he has never observed that kind of pressure situation, a blowout can be difficult to recover from.

THE PRECOCIOUS PLAYER

On a rainy, overcast morning in Manhattan, Nick Bollettieri introduced the 12-year-old that he, and other insiders in the world of fast-track tennis, expect will become the next child prodigy. Monika Seles, a native of Yugoslavia who'd begun playing only five years earlier, rallied on a midget court laid over the floor of the ballroom of the Roosevelt Hotel. Ranked number one in the world in her age group, Seles was already taking sets off male college players at Bollettieri's Florida tennis school. In the world of tennis, *that* news travels fast. Even Washington agent-tournament director Donald Dell had caught the buzz in the air: a few weeks earlier, Dell had made a special southern visit to see Seles for himself.

Five feet tall, her brown hair cut short above her shoulders, she hardly cut an imposing figure. Neither had Austin or Jaeger, Bollettieri reminded his audience of teaching professionals and United States Tennis Association officials, gathered together for the 1986 National Tennis Teachers Conference.

"Monika has," Bollettieri said, holding a microphone, "all the strokes, and a full-court game."

A few feet away, the young girl angled crosscourt backhands that her 18-year-old brother, Zoltan—the Yugoslav national junior champion—could barely return.

It's much too soon to describe Seles as a phenomenon; after all, she will not be able to even enter professional tournaments until 1988, when she turns 14. The Seles story is, however, instructive. For parents concerned that their child may not be developing in the proper environment, Monika Seles offers encouragement. For parents worried that their lack of a tennis background could cripple their child's chances of success, the Seles story is inspirational. And for parents intimidated by the apparent high cost of creating a champion, the Seles saga is, well, enlightening. For it has not cost Monika or her brother much at all to train at the Bollettieri academy. Those expenses have been underwritten by sponsors and by Bollettieri himself. It is, they figure, an investment in the future.

A future that, by all rights, shouldn't exist. Unlike tennis in Czechoslovakia and even, lately, the Soviet

Union, Yugoslav tennis is disorganized. There is no strong national federation with the means to subsidize regional and local coaches. There is no national league, which in other European countries provides the structure for most junior competition. No, what Monika Seles had going for her was a father who'd been a top national athlete—but not a tennis player—and who had the kind of job that allowed him to make his own hours and spend time with his son and daughter on the tennis court.

"My father started playing with my brother first," Monika recalled in Florida one evening after her three-hour workout. "He had never played, but was a national track star."

"The triple jump," added Zoltan, who stays with Monika when she's training in the United States and participates in her coaching. "He was a sportsman all his life. But he never played tennis. I can help Monika more as a player than my father can. But when I don't know something, then he helps me."

Karol Seles learned his tennis strokes out of an instructional booklet he bought after watching Bjorn Borg win at Wimbledon. As a cartoonist for magazines both in Yugoslavia and abroad, Seles could work more or less when he pleased. That was crucial in a country where finding a free court could take time and effort. In the Seleses' home city of Novi Sad, population 200,000, there were only, by Zoltan's count, eight courts.

"When Monika turned nine," said Zoltan, who himself began at twelve and six years later was his country's 18-and-under champion, "she'd never played on a court. Her hitting until then had been in a parking lot."

Both Seles children agree that the key to their success was that their father never put any pressure on them to win.

"My father learned in his own mind," Monika said. "He learned from reading and from watching. I want to be the best, and my models are Martina Navratilova, Chris Evert, and Mats Wilander. But my father had no models. He knew about sport, and about pressure. And he knew to keep the sport fun."

And in 1988, at the ripe old age of fourteen, Monika Seles will have the chance to test that formula for success on the pro circuit.

"My goal?" said the twelve-year-old. "To be number one. The best."

ONE PRO'S PERSPECTIVE

Terry Phelps has a sense of what Monika Seles may eventually go through. Phelps was ranked twenty-first in the world midway through 1986, the third year on the professional women's circuit for the Larchmont, New York, native. She'd turned professional just before her seventeenth birthday, a little over a year after winning the 18-and-under division of the Orange Bowl tournament; in that tournament, she'd upset then top-ranked Marianne Werdel, a girl she'd never beaten. Although Phelps had yet to match her junior success, she was making a living, something many juniors turned pro could envy. By the end of the 1986 tour, her earnings would be comfortably in six figures.

Phelps's perspective on the pressures put on good juniors by their parents is interesting, for she's neither at the top of her profession nor on the fringes, outside looking in. Here is her view from the center of the beast, the heart of the competitive pressures that, ultimately, drive the junior game.

"My parents had other lives besides tennis," Phelps said one warm, summer morning as she rested on a bench next to a private court in Chestnut Hill, a suburb of Boston, Massachusetts, where the United States Professional Men's Tennis Championships are held annually at the Longwood Cricket Club. Although those matches were being held just a mile away, the lanky six-footer had little interest. She'd followed her coach to New England, hoping to get in some extra training while he supervised the handful of players he had in the Longwood draw. "A lot of the kids," she continued, "when they're twelve years old, their parents devote their lives to making their girl number one in the world.

"That seems a little much. My parents would push me hard, but then we'd take time off, and do other things. My whole life wasn't tennis. I never thought I was going to be a pro until I turned sixteen. Some people have it in their minds when they're ten. If they don't make it, they're frustrated, or worse.

"The game was easy for me to get involved in. We lived by a public park, with courts, and both my parents played. At first I just hit with them. Then, when I was seven, they enrolled me in a little local summer program. At nine, I started getting private lessons, once a week, after school. The next year I started playing tournaments, and was playing in the national 12-and-unders by the end of that year. I always wanted to play, and don't recall them forcing me. If they had, I'd probably have rebelled.

"Recently, I've found that I have to work on my concentration more. A couple of years ago, my mom noticed I was always looking around in the stands during my matches. I'd play two games well at that time, then one not so well. That hadn't been a problem for me in the juniors.

"There, when I was developing my game, my dad would give me a few pointers. You know, play each point at a time, things like that. I concentrated better than others when I was a junior. Some girls would have terrible tempers, screaming, going hysterical. I was shy. And, it turned out, I was doing something right. Since then I've learned that getting mad can affect your play for at least the next couple of points.

"Here's an example. I was playing in the qualifying [round] of the Virginia Slims in Chicago a couple of years ago, and my opponent went nuts. I thought she was going to weep. 'There's no way I can lose,' I told myself. She was throwing her racquet against the fence on every line call. McEnroe's the only one I've ever seen who isn't affected negatively by anger. He gets upset, then seems to hit two aces. How he does that, I don't know.

"My attitude towards pressure is: if you're throwing up with nervousness, that's not much fun. I try not to think, just play. Once you begin to worry about losing, that your ranking's going to be hurt, you're in trouble. When the match is over, forget about it. Go on to other things.

"The pressure to turn pro is touching younger and younger girls. Some are quitting school at thirteen, and taking correspondence courses. If you ask me, that's sick. I was almost seventeen when I turned pro. College? I don't know. I don't even think about it right now. I guess I'd like to. It's good to go. But if I finish tennis at twenty-six, I can't see going back to college. I know the United States Tennis Association study suggests that would be a long career, but when I was sixteen and seventeen, I just played one tournament a month. I don't think I'll burn out. There are a lot of twenty-seven-year-olds playing."

AND A WORD FROM SOME PARENTS

Chris Evert Lloyd's mother, Colette Evert, wasn't surprised that her youngest daughter, Clare, didn't turn professional. Like older sisters Chrissie and Jeanne, Clare Evert had been a nationally ranked junior, and some—including her mother—thought she hit the ball harder than Chrissie. But, as Colette Evert told *World Tennis* interviewer Neil Amdur, daughter Clare never embraced competition the way Chris and Jeanne had. "She didn't seem to catch on to her opponent's weaknesses, and this is something that is in-born," Colette Evert said. "She would drop-shot ten times, and the other person would make the point nine times, and she would still keep on drop-shotting."

A parent's sensitivity toward each child, and the child's competitive spirit, is crucial to success in junior tennis, Colette Evert suggested. And the game has changed considerably since Chris Evert shocked the fans at the United States Open at Forest Hills, New York, in 1971 by making it to the semifinals.

"There is more pressure on the children," Evert said. "Unless a child shows at age twelve some remarkable ability, like a Mary Joe Fernandez, my advice would be to stay in the junior ranks, travel, and maybe go to college. There are so many more opportunities now for a child who is good to remain an amateur that didn't exist when Chrissie was little."

Bill Barber, for one, recognizes that. Barber, an engineer, has raised a family of nationally ranked juniors in Maryland, where on weekends he organizes junior tournaments and calls lines or sits in the chair at the occasional pro tournament (the latter a role he played at the mixed doubles final of the 1986 United States Open). Barber's section, or region, is the Mid-Atlantic, a rather small area encompassing Maryland, Virginia, the District of Columbia, and part of West Virginia. "At the moment," Barber said in midsummer of 1986, "we've got 5,000 registered juniors in the section, but only 600 are active."

For these Mid-Atlantic juniors, the rankings and endorsements—that is, which juniors are nominated to play in the national junior events—are dictated by computerized standings. Without an endorsement from the section a junior lives in, that player cannot enter a national tournament and thereby cannot hope to receive a national ranking. Barber, and other parents, say politics can play a significant role in those endorsements.

The Mid-Atlantic holds fifty junior tournaments annually per age group, and a junior must play in at least five to be ranked. One of the five must be a specially designated national qualifier event, and there are four of those spaced over the year.

In any given age group in the mid-Atlantic, only four players are endorsed for national tournaments. This contrasts with a region like the Southern section, which includes every southern state from North Carolina to Alabama. (Only Florida is separate, that hotbed of junior tennis having its own section.) Although the Southern section endorses twenty juniors per age group to play national events, the pressure in that section is greater.

"They've got close to 50,000 registered juniors," Barber figured, "and there is only one national qualifying tournament there each year. If you're sick, or injured that week, you've got no shot."

For Bill Barber and his three children—Bonnie, Cindy, and Billy—succeeding in junior tennis was a matter of careful budgeting, realistic expectations, and enthusiastic support from both Mother and Father. For Bonnie, who was ranked nationally in every age group beginning at the 12s, the experience was capped by a four-year scholarship to Boston University, where she captained the tennis team. Cindy, at 17, was coming off a year where she was ranked in the section top 10 in singles, and nationally in the top 20 in doubles. A semifinal finish in the national 18-and-under grass court doubles capped the summer, and college, too, seemed a certainty for her. Billy, playing in the 16-and-unders at Kalamazoo, surprised both himself and coach Bob Pass by winning three rounds. College coaches circulating around the Michigan campus made a point of introducing themselves.

"The expenses to do this can be astonishing," Barber said. "The academies now cost as much as $1,800 a month. But parents think they need them for their son or daughter to become a top pro. They see others do it, and think, 'Gee, if I don't, my kid won't keep up with his friends.' At first, the kids were just going in the summer. But now it's year-round."

For the Barbers, the academies—financially—were out of the question. So was taking a coach with them to tournaments. That would mean paying the coach's expenses, something Bill Barber couldn't afford to do.

"We'd look for ways to cut the money," Barber said. "Bill and Cindy would share an hour lesson a week, and altogether they'd only play twice a week. Other kids I'd see, kids they were playing against, would have three weekly lessons, go to five or six different clinics, buy the best clothes, and take their coach on the road. That adds up quickly, to anywhere from $10,000 to $20,000 a year."

The Barbers never spent more than $5,000 annually, even when all three kids were competing. Of course, they were fortunate in that racquet, sneaker, and clothing manufacturers eventually had all the Barber juniors on one free list or another. For Billy, who receives a Nike package every month or so, that can amount to several thousand dollars' worth of clothing over a year.

The other cost-cutter used by the Barbers is free housing. Most major junior tournaments arrange for players to stay with local families, if they wish. Years ago, the pro circuit offered the same arrangement, but as the money's grown, that amenity's become obsolete. Many tournaments, indeed, offer free hotel rooms now to entice players.

For Bonnie Barber, the free housing was a mixed blessing.

"At the Philadelphia tournament," she remembered, "we stayed with a family, very wealthy, who wouldn't let us into most of the house. We could go into our bedroom, the living room, and the kitchen. The girl with me spilled a drink on the bedspread, and our hostess went nuts. She screamed that she was going to have to have everything dry-cleaned."

"When they were younger," Bill Barber shrugged, gesturing at his two daughters, "the kids didn't like the housing. But we had to take advantage of it. When there's an event far away, like a Kalamazoo or Houston, the kids go on their own."

The independence of the Barber children helped with the pressures of the game, but not as much as Bill Barber's experience in running junior tennis tournaments himself. There he saw just what pressure can do, up close and personal, at the first tournament he ran.

"It was in Claverly, Maryland, a little club," Barber said, "and there were two little girls playing each other. Both their fathers were watching from the side, and one father became convinced the other girl was cheating. He said something about it to the other father, and the next thing I knew, the cheater's father had picked up an aluminum lawn chair and was beating the guy over the head with it."

There were other epiphanies: the day a father threatened to punch out a club member because the member had asked the junior, playing a match on a neighboring court, to be quiet; the afternoon at Norfolk, Virginia, when one father began to slap his daughter after she lost a match he thought she should have won; a son abandoned by his father after a match, with no way to get home; and two mothers clawing each other with fingernails after one had made fun of the other's daughter's racquets. No, it wasn't difficult for Bill Barber to come to the conclusion that the most important thing he could do for his three children was to keep the pressure off.

"I realized that the kids are dealing with the parents' psyches too," Barber said. "Those kids either seemed to grow up fast, or to drop out. The parents were losing perspective. I didn't want it to happen to me."

Or to the children. Cindy Barber remembers when she figured out exactly what her father was talking about.

"I was in the 12s," she said, "and I was playing a girl who was top-ranked at the time. I'd never beaten her, but, this time, I was up 5–4 in the first set and I was serving.

" 'I can't play any more,' she told me. Then her eyes glazed over, and she passed out, right on the court."

TENNIS BRATS

Precocious players can easily become tennis "brats," youngsters whose success has come to so dominate the family life that parents are reluctant to confront them on even the most egregious behavior: rudeness, temper, even cheating. The amount of money it takes to produce a top player, the lure of rewards—both financial benefits and notoriety—the glamour associated with the travel can create a sense in some parents that any kind of behavior must be tolerated, lest discipline bring a winning streak to an end.

Sarah Jones (not her real name) had developed a reputation as a brat long before she began to be thrown out of tournaments. A nationally ranked teenager, Jones would berate her opponents, calling their good shots "lucky" and sneering "you're a hook" after each close call that went against her.

Her mother, Vicki, not an athlete, had become enchanted with the possibility of Sarah's becoming a champion, perhaps eventually turning pro. Her father was less involved, and he didn't travel with Sarah, an only child, and his wife to matches. He wouldn't hear Sarah, as she came off the court, turn to her mother and say, "Get out of my life. You've got no right to talk to me."

Vicki Jones rationalized Sarah's behavior as acceptable because Sarah was winning. Yet Sarah, a ruthless competitor who was willing to cheat on line calls if she felt her opponent was doing the same, eventually began estranging tournament officials. After Sarah was defaulted in one important match, Vicki finally concluded that something was wrong. Yet her solution was to focus on Sarah's on-court behavior, to teach her a more emotionally controlled game. That paid off, with Sarah capturing a major holiday invitational event although she wasn't seeded. But off-court, Sarah remained the same. And so did Vicki.

"Are you practicing enough?" Vicki would ask as Sarah brushed by. She should have been demanding, "Why are you treating me this way?"

Sarah Jones, like other tennis brats, had developed an inflated, artificial ego. As long as she was playing, she could get away with virtually anything. Although the rest of the tennis community perceived Sarah as horribly self-centered, her mother felt trapped. And this is typical of parents of tennis brats. They believe their children are under great stress—which they indeed are—and they decide any criticism or discipline would only add to that. So they turn their backs.

In doing so, however, they're making a sad mistake. The emotional development of the child demands a strong parental role, and that includes discipline. Parents can't permit their fear of breaking the cycle of winning to cause them to tank on their children.

THE SUCCESSFUL PARENT IS MENTALLY TOUGH

Parents who learn to keep the pressure off their children, who involve themselves positively in the competitive situations their sons and daughters find themselves in— parents like Colette Evert, Bill Barber, and the parents of Monika Seles and Terry Phelps—are as mentally tough as any player. This is important to keep in mind, and the aspects of this kind of mental toughness are worth reviewing.

A mentally tough parent has *emotional control*. A parent lacking mental toughness will show that in one of three ways: tanking, loss of temper, or fear. In tanking, parents on the sidelines will give up on their child during and after a loss. This is no less tanking than the child's giving up himself. A tanking parent will lose interest, taking the attitude that the child is choosing to behave in a manner that's unacceptable, and that the parent, therefore, can dismiss him.

This attitude can have a devastating effect, undercutting the child's ability to play his own game, and develop his own on-court solutions. The child can see that Mom and Dad are more interested, more connected, when the junior follows their advice instead of acting on his own, and when he wins instead of loses. If the child asserts his independence—and the parents haven't prepared for that—he can see his parents detach themselves and tank.

Or the parents can lose their temper. When their child loses, they'll turn pessimistic, or aggressive. They'll pace the sideline, boiling. Or get upset at home. Maybe on the drive home, or later in the week, they'll turn a cold shoulder toward the child. Whatever the case, they're eschewing the formula for success: empathy and patience.

Finally, the parent can grow frightened over a match's outcome. In a sense, this is the most positive of the three negative states, for here, anyway, the parent is involved and caring. But showing fear, modeling nervousness and tension, can distract the child if he notices the parent's behavior. When he does, he's likely to become more afraid. A good coach will never demonstrate nervousness, and a mentally tough parent shouldn't either.

Mentally tough parents want to stay within themselves, "in the center of the circle" if you will. Their Ideal Performance State should exhibit, on the surface, the same qualities their son's or daughter's does: relaxation, calmness, plenty of energy. The mentally tough parent stays engaged throughout a match, regardless of its outcome. If a mentally tough parent gets nervous, he disguises his fear. The child needs to sense from the parent that everything is going to be okay, no matter what happens on the court. With one exception: if a parent observes unethical behavior from his junior, whether it's cheating, berating an opponent, or abusing an official, the parent *must* show disapproval, anger, and frustration.

Simply put, if parents aren't emotionally tough, they'll get eaten up by the sport and its pressures. They'll become victims.

A bare-bones checklist for developing mental toughness includes the following:

- *The key is emotional control.*

- *Parents must see things clearly.*

- *Parents must not allow themselves to get overwhelmed by the glamour, the money, and the hoopla.*

- *Parents must be organized, and disciplined. Just as a player can't let himself be overwhelmed by the court conditions, or a cheating opponent, so must a parent not become overwhelmed by the logistics and expenses of training, travel, and the tournaments themselves.*

6 CHOOSING A COACH

Twenty minutes after a first-round, straight-set loss, Gigi Fernandez looked elated to the reporters eager to interview her. She had, after all, stretched Martina Navratilova to her fullest in the first set, breaking the world's best twice and fighting back from 3–5 to 5 all.

Fernandez, the beautiful, 22-year-old Puerto Rican native who'd seriously slumped after breaking into the top 25 of the women's computer ranking list, could hardly be depressed about her performance. After all, just a few months earlier, she couldn't have even gotten into the main draw of this, the $350,000 Virginia Slims Championships of New England. Her ranking had dropped well below 100, and her confidence was shot.

"The players had lost respect for my game," Fernandez said, sitting behind a cluster of microphones in a small interview room deep in the bowels of the Centrum, a concrete auditorium in Worcester, Massachusetts. "Not that that surprised me. There was nothing to respect."

Fernandez's crisis had come three years into her professional career. Unlike many of her peers, she'd played in college (at Clemson University), and she'd lost a national championship final to Beth Herr in 1983. After a year of victories on the satellite circuit—which offers small prize money in fringe locations—Fernandez qualified for, and eventually reached the finals of, the Virginia Slims event in Newport, Rhode Island. There she'd lost, ironically enough, to Navratilova. Afterward, Navratilova wrote her a note.

"You need some more determination," Fernandez remembered it reading.

"I told her she was overweight," recalled Navratilova at her press conference.

Whatever the text, the message had been received. At the time, Fernandez was barely on the women's computer list—around 520 was her recollection. By 1985, however, Fernandez had risen to 22. Navratilova, for one, noticed. She invited Fernandez to play doubles with her at the Virginia Slims in Washington, and the odd couple won.

Fernandez felt she'd reached a plateau with her game, a level that her coach, Don Usher, couldn't push her through. Usher was a fine tactician, she knew, but at 44 he couldn't push her around the court the way, say, a Mike Estep could work Navratilova. It was time for a change. Fernandez left Usher and began training with younger men: Joe Brandi, Andy Johnson, Benny Sims. "I thought I needed someone to work out with, to get me in shape," she said. But as her ranking plummeted, she decided she'd made a mistake.

"Actually, I was thinking about retiring," Fernandez admitted. She asked Usher if he'd work with her again.

The benefits were immediate. As the tour swung through Asia, Fernandez won three consecutive events, winning more matches in three weeks than she'd won in the previous year and a half. The difference, she concluded, was almost entirely mental. And Usher's return, more than any specific coaching he'd done, had made that difference.

"Confidence," Fernandez concluded, smiling. "That's what it's all about. Confidence."

On that point, Navratilova told the assembled reporters, she had to agree.

"When you're not sure of yourself," the women's champion said, "you get tentative. And *that* feeds on itself."

GETTING THE RIGHT COACH FOR THE JOB

If a Gigi Fernandez, the twenty-second-best woman tennis player in the world at the time, can not fathom her coaching needs, then it stands to reason that this is no simple task for the parent of the beginning junior. Indeed, there is no set formula to choosing a coach. The best one can do is to explore the options carefully and find a teacher who, at least, will give your child a passion for the game.

If a mistake is made, well, there are other coaches. Just ask Gigi Fernandez.

Tennis, particularly the junior game, can sneak up on parents. We've noted this point before, but it's worth repeating. The expenses, the travel, but most of all the innate pressure of the game itself can seriously strain the relationship between parent and child. An effective coach can not only train a young player to hit the proper strokes and develop court strategy, but can also enhance the parent-child relationship, buffering the tension that can result when Mom and Dad and junior lose perspective over the game they're supporting and playing.

Not that a coach is a cure-all, by any means. The following is a letter from a top junior girl enrolled at a tennis academy who was trying to come to grips with the pressure a parent was putting on her.

> Mom,
>
> How are you doing? I'm good. I'm studying hard since I can't play. Mom, I love you so much, but I have to talk to you . . . I think you're worrying about my tennis too much.
>
> When I go to play tournaments, you're happy and everything's great, but when I lose, you won't eat, sleep, or talk. It gets me so mad. I get hurt and start to hate the game. The way you are always talking tennis and telling me what to work on, I feel so much pressure. I have my coaches here that help me with that.
>
> When you talk like this, it makes it harder for me to play. If all of us can't be happy with how and what I'm doing I might as well quit playing tennis. Mom, I want to be happy when I play and I want to play because I love to play and I love the game. You've helped me a lot with my tennis, but

now I'm growing up and I want to do it by myself without having you always saying what I need to work on.

We talk about different things but we always talk about my tennis. Mom, I love you very much. I'm afraid to mail this letter because I don't want you to be mad at me, and I don't want to hurt you. But I feel that I have to do this for the both of us. . . .

This young player, obviously, is struggling. And her coaches are, to a certain extent, helpless. For many coaches, however, keeping parents involved in their child, and the child's game, is just as substantial a problem.

Parents unable to instill a love of the game in their children may turn to the outsider to accomplish that. This generally happens with young novices, children who've not yet learned the fundamentals. Older players, juniors who've tested their feet in competitive waters, are coming to coaches at a different stage, with different needs. And for these children, a coach may be a means of escaping their parents.

"Parents simply get too close," says Harvard University men's tennis coach David Fish. "It's similar to the real estate business. A realtor will tell you, 'Once I care too much about a property, I stop making good decisions.' Parents are in the same boat. They want to make all the difficulties easy, thinking they have only one chance. Parents talk about removing pressure, but often they speak a lie. Everyone knows how to speak the lines, but their actions send a different message. There's a conflict there, between real values, and what is transmitted to the kids.

"When I win, and throw my racquet, I'm excused. When I throw the racquet, and lose, there's no excusing."

There are three basic stages at which a parent and child can find themselves choosing a coach: the early years, the first years of competition, and the top levels of junior tennis. Obviously, the vast majority of children playing tennis see only one or possibly two coaches. The first teaches strokes, and the second—likely at the high-school level—oversees a fairly rudimentary type of competition. A second, smaller group of children will graduate into junior tennis, often under the coaching of a local club professional. And the third group—children whose goal is, at the least, to play college tennis—may wind up with a coach who not only works with ranked players, but travels with them as well.

In the early years, setting a proper perspective is a priority for any coach. Beginners need to be introduced to tennis in a way that imparts a love of the game. The best coaches at this level do that creatively, much as an elementary-school teacher can instill a love for reading, or a passion for arithmetic. These tennis teachers have a charisma, a Mary Poppins quality. Like a Pied Piper, they're followed by the kids they teach, and like the PBS's Mister Rogers, they're sensitive to a child's needs for affection and attention. Tennis, they believe, is a means to meet those needs, a way to connect emotionally with children.

Because this is a special gift, a parent cannot assume any teaching professional who works with young children will have it. Parents have to be willing to do a bit of investigation on their own: to go to a clinic or a lesson before enrolling their child and study the interaction of the teacher and the pupils.

Some of the questions a parent should ask while watching are, are the children excited? Are they enjoying themselves? Is the teacher prone to criticism, or is he encouraging? Is the teaching pro only attracted to children with a lot of natural talent? Does he appear to be out to produce a superstar?

What the parent wants is someone who treats the students equally—who has a feel for the game's fundamentals, yes, but more importantly, a feel for the children.

The second level of coaching comes later, after a passion for the game has been instilled. By this point, most children will be ready to compete, or actually competing. Since the existing body of psychological research—and the junior players themselves—are not enthusiastic about match play prior to 10 years old, this level typically will first be reached between the ages of 10 and 12. For late starters, it can come in the mid- to late teens.

At this point, parents should find a coach who has a keen understanding of the game's fundamentals. Mini-tennis, baseball tennis (where a youngster throws a tennis ball around a court instead of hitting it), and games of that sort are no longer especially relevant. Because coaches gain reputations based on their strengths (and weaknesses), the parent should again investigate on his own. How a coach teaches individual strokes, whether the teaching pro had good coaching himself—these are background aspects a parent should concern himself with.

WHAT ARE THE QUALIFICATIONS?

Parents should also research carefully when choosing a coach for their top players. Many parents assume that, because a coach had a good record as a player, the competitive experience will translate into coaching expertise. This isn't so. Indeed, many great players have had little success coaching. On the one hand, exceptional players are often gifted athletes who were able to pick up the game with great ease. And, on the other, they may be afflicted with an unwillingness to give up the center stage, and may be trying to extend their championship seasons through their protégés. Bill Tilden, who dominated men's tennis in the twenties, was a classic example. As a coach, noted his biographer, Frank Deford in *Big Bill Tilden*, Tilden "was unrelenting and dogmatic, hard on conditioning, and even innovative in some respects; but he never psychologically committed himself to teaching."

Deford writes that he tracked down a former pupil, California businessman Noel Brown, who related the following. The words ring true today for many circuit players turned coaches. "Bill's great failing—at least as he grew older—was that he couldn't understand his time and place in life. Noel Brown was a tournament player, but now, in this place and time [Brown raps his desk] Noel Brown is a business executive. Bill Tilden never let go of the fact that he was no longer a great champion. He carried it all through his life. On the one hand, he was trying to find an extension of himself, to continue as champion through myself and these various other young players. It was his mother-and-father instinct. But, on the other hand, he could never follow that instinct completely, do what was best for him and them, and be a real teaching pro. He did the teaching in a half-assed way just to carry himself along. Make no mistake: Bill Tilden was always playing. He was always a player in his own mind. He could never find himself out here as a coach."

An ex-champion will often teach the way he played, too, refusing to consider either that his junior students lack the physical maturity to emulate his game, or that his biomechanics were, in fact, poorly executed. (Vic Braden, the tennis teaching pro turned psychologist currently based in California, points out that he will confront touring pros who insist that they "roll the wrist over" by videotaping their strokes and showing—in slow motion—that the wrist roll occurs after the ball has left the racquet and, in fact, has no effect on the stroke. If they aren't given the Braden treatment, though, these pros will turn later to coaching and insist that their pupils learn to roll their wrists to hit topspin, a pointless exercise.)

There are two organizations that teaching professionals can join: the United States Professional Tennis Association, based in Saddlebrook, Florida, and the United States Professional Tennis Registry, created by Dennis Van der Meer and run out of Hilton Head, South Carolina. Both the USPTA and the USPTR rank their members on different levels, according to how much formal training they've had and the results on various tests. At the USPTR, Van der Meer's staff conducts a teaching clinic for members called "TU I," has to be one of the best single experiences available in this country for players learning to be coaches. All USPTR teachers have to participate in this clinic. The USPTA offers regular training programs nationwide conducted by its most experienced and renowned members. Philosophically, the USPTA offers a more diversified, eclectic approach to teaching, whereas the USPTR strictly follows the Van der Meer method.

Discovering whether a coach has had formal training is important, but there are other questions a parent should ask, too. Does the coach attend regional and national conventions or conferences? Does the teaching pro get involved with local seminars? Many country-club professionals don't, and as result, they have lost touch with the game's structure and technological changes. Their attitude tends to be "I know it all." But tennis is no different from any other profession, be it laser technology or toy manufacturing: the best people stay on the cutting edge.

Only after the parent has established that the coach is involved with the system—that he goes to conferences, that he's been certified, that he's familiar with the game's structure as well as its strokes—should the parent then factor in whether the coach was a great player himself. Of course, here too there are exceptions. When Hana Mandlikova and her father sought out Betty Stove, the Dutch star of the seventies, and asked her to become Hana's coach, whether Stove was certified was inconsequential. Mandlikova was looking for someone to guide her through the complexities of the women's tour, which Stove was eminently qualified to do. And those exceptions hold true at the top junior levels in America: parents of players who are already ranked may be looking for coaches whose experience is available for hire. Great rewards—equipment, travel opportunities, college scholarships—can come from a modestly improved national ranking. That, in turn, can derive from a couple of good wins. The system in this country puts great emphasis on obtaining an edge over one's opponent, whether or not that edge translates, in fact, into excellence on the court. Winning is what is important, and coaches may condone inappropriate behavior to realize it.

If a parent with extremely high expectations for a son or daughter retains a coach who had moderate success as a player, and who has never coached a great player—someone with a high national ranking—that parent is probably running a risk. And not an uncommon one. A coach often takes a junior to the highest level the coach himself played at, and never goes beyond. The obstacles—unfamiliarity with the tournaments, perhaps even a lack of strategic expertise—can block coach as well as player. In other countries, this may not be the case. Both Czechoslovakia and Sweden, for example, have various levels of coaching, and a junior progresses through a system that begins at the local club level and continues to top international junior play. These countries have come to understand that it's nearly impossible for one coach to bring a young player from a beginner to a world-class level.

Why should parents and players anticipate changing coaches as a player develops?

Personality conflict, for one. A child begins the game before he turns 10, and for any coach to be able to stay with that junior, month after month, year after year, until he graduates from the junior circuit, places impossible demands on the coach's psychological skills. Not that coaches don't expect loyalty. They do. But from the player's perspective, change is often a necessity. A child grows and matures; a coach may not. If a junior becomes bored

115

with his coach, and his coach's attitude toward the game, burnout may be just a tournament away.

Nevertheless, a top player is a coach's prize—a meal ticket, if you will, to the game's highest levels. Just as major equipment and clothing manufacturers will compete with each other to have a top junior or collegian playing with their racquet, or wearing their shoes, socks, and T-shirts, so may coaches try to entice players to stay with them, either waiving lesson fees or offering to accompany a player to a tournament at no charge. It's important, therefore, for a parent to look for emotional stability in a coach for an accomplished junior.

Shared values, someone who'll deal with morals and ethics and character—a coach at this level ought to be able to perform as a parental surrogate. And a parent whose son or daughter will be on the road with the coach has every right to inquire into the coach's background. In mental toughness terms, the parent ought to know how effective a coach is in establishing his own Ideal Performance State: how does the coach respond to a crisis? Can the coach maintain control? Does the coach keep the game in perspective?

As tough as tennis is for the player, it may be tougher to coach. Burnout is common—coaches spend a great deal of time on the court, and they can become both physically and mentally exhausted. A tired coach can feel he's trapped in the game. One former junior coach recalled that he knew it was time to leave when he began waking in the middle of the night in a sweat.

"I kept seeing millions of balls," he said, "and I had to hit all of them. It was a nightmare I couldn't shake."

116

When a coach burns out, the students suffer, too. The coach doesn't care any more, and he puts less into the lesson. He loses his patience and is quick to criticize. In the end, a burned-out coach is at one extreme or the other: totally apathetic, or quick to strike negatively, a rattlesnake in white shorts.

A parent sensitive to this problem will talk to a prospective coach before committing his child. He'll find out how much time the coach is spending on the court daily, and whether the coach has ways of supplementing his income off-court. If a coach is hitting balls for 40 hours a week, or more, that coach is potentially in trouble. A parent should also be willing to inquire about a coach's personal life: whether he's married, whether there are events placing him under great stress, whether he's under a financial burden. Discreet inquiries around his club can often elicit the kind of information that makes it easy to decide whether to make the commitment or not.

SUSAN SLOANE: A HAPPY COINCIDENCE

Luck and chance can play an important part in finding the right coach. The pairing of Susan Sloane and Fritz Nau proves that parents may find the best coach right under their noses, even if that coach has never played a tournament match in his life.

In 1976, a truck driver named Fritz Nau happened to be passing through Lexington, Kentucky, when he noticed a sign advertising the opening of a new indoor tennis club. Nau had been a college basketball player, but had turned to

117

tennis, a sport he'd never played as a child, after graduation. He'd wanted to stay in shape, and had enrolled in Dennis Van der Meer's tennis professional course in South Carolina at Hilton Head.

Now, as he rolled through the Kentucky city, Nau thought he might be able to get his exercise, and get paid, too.

The club hired the blond over-six-footer as an assistant, assigning him clinics for the youngest players. Among his students were a fourteen-year-old and her six-year-old sister. The elementary school student intrigued Nau, because she didn't seem to miss. Her name, he quickly learned, was Susan Sloane.

For Susan Sloane, the opening of the club that winter was a godsend. Kentucky was buried in a season-long freak snow, and every week, it seemed, school would be canceled for two or three days at a stretch. Susan would hang around the club with her mother and older sister, playing with anyone who'd agree to go on the court.

"I was just in love with the game," Susan remembers. "It was all I wanted to do."

Nau felt Susan was something special, yet he couldn't be certain. After all, he'd never played competitively, and none of his other pupils was playing tournaments, even at the local level. But after nine months of twice-a-week clinics, he agreed to let Susan enter a 10-and-under event. She did well, then nearly beat the top-ranked 12-and-under player in the state. By the middle of her seventh year, Susan Sloane had a state ranking. At 8, she did well in the sectionals, and qualified for the national 12-and-under tournaments. Her parents, thinking she was too young, held her back. The next year she won the 12-and-under division in the nine-state region and advanced to the nationals. Only one other player—Mary Joe Fernandez, now a touring pro—was as young as Sloane.

"Susan lost in the first round, and I began to think I'd made a mistake," Nau says. "After all, she was still the first tournament player I'd had. But in the back draw, against top players much older than her, Susan won five rounds." The uncertainty passed.

When Sloane was 11, she was ranked first in the country in the 12s. The next year, she played the 14s, and ended the season as the country's fourth best. At 13, she was playing two age groups—the 14s and the 16s, where she finished the season ranked one and two, respectively, in the two groups. By the time she was 14, Sloane was playing the 18s, and at 15 was ranked third in that group.

Nau's strategy, early on, was to expose his pupil to as much of the tennis world as he and Sloane's parents could afford. He took her to clinics run by coaches such as Vic Braden and arranged for private lessons with the likes of Pancho Segura. "I wanted to give her a feel for the people on the national level," Nau says. "Segura was major. I was using his tactics in practice, making sure that the last thing she did each day was to work on her serve, that kind of structure." With Susan's mother, Pat, the three would travel the national circuit.

In Susan's mind, Pat Sloane's support was the key. "She's the one who goes to every tournament," Susan says. "She's around the game more than my father, although they're both interested. And from what I've seen, I've got the best tennis parents. If I've lost, or played badly, my mother will offer constructive criticism. But I see other parents yelling at their children, not making any sense at all, even when they've played badly, yet won. My mother's always positive, and that's important. If you're on the court, knowing that your parents or your coach—whoever it might be—will get upset if you play poorly, it's got to be impossible to concentrate. Especially if you win anyway. I mean, if you can play badly and *win*, well, that's a great accomplishment."

Eventually, the junior system left little in the way of a challenge for Susan Sloane. From age 11 until she turned professional in 1986, Sloane's competition consisted of the same handful of girls. International play was drastically limited—the United States Tennis Association won't underwrite travel for a player not ranked in the 18-and-under division, and Susan wasn't eligible to play up that high until 1985. In the meantime, other girls her age—Argentina's Gabriela Sabatini, Hungary's Katrina Maleeva—were competing throughout the world.

"The way it's set up in this country," Nau says, "you have to wait for that 18s ranking. But when she was 12, there were some international tournaments (they've since been discontinued for the Americans), and Susan and Stephanie Rehe and Mary Joe Fernandez (who also turned professional) were beating those girls. What happens in the United States is that you wind up playing the same girls over and over again. By the time they meet the great foreign players four or five years later, the foreign girls have significant experience at the professional level. In fact, I don't think Susan would have turned pro if she'd been able to play these girls."

Susan Sloane more or less agrees. "I pretty much did all I could in the juniors," she says. "After six years of nationals, it was starting to get old. Real old."

The relationship between Nau and Sloane grew stale too. They began to bicker during practice and eventually sought the advice of other coaches on how to continue. At the end of 1985, Nau stopped working with Sloane on court and joined the Bollettieri Tennis Academy staff. Sloane became a pupil of Bollettieri's. Then, a year later, Bollettieri reunited the two. Nau was put in charge of Sloane's workouts.

After a year of distance, Nau could recognize a change in her attitude. "Like many top juniors," Nau recalls, "Susan had reached a position where everything she did was being judged in terms of winning and losing. She — like many, many others — had lost sight of what aspects of her game needed developing. At age 11, when you're number one in the country, it's tough to work on coming to net, on the underspin backhand, and it's almost impossible to change grips. Once you're at the top, a slip, and you're written off. It happens so quickly. So, even when she was young, it was difficult to work on the things she'd need two years later.

"But now, at 16, she's more open to change than she was seven years ago. In the juniors, she could say, 'I'm Susie Sloane, this is the way I play, and I'm gonna stick it in your ear.' That doesn't work in the pros."

For Susan Sloane and her family, and for Fritz Nau, the journey through the juniors had a happy ending. For others, that isn't always the case.

ONE MOTHER'S TALE

Late in 1985, an official of the New Jersey Tennis Association—a mother of three whose daughter had been ranked in the state throughout her junior career, but who had never broken into the upper echelons of national junior play—wrote us, describing the experiences she, as a tennis parent, had had in wrestling with the problems of competition we've described in this book. Like many other parents, she'd been frustrated by the pressure of the game on both her and her daughter, the politics and favoritism influencing which juniors got recommended, or endorsed, for national tournaments, and the difficulties in choosing coaches. The following names have been changed.

"Our family also had several experiences with teaching pros," the New Jersey official noted. "There are many good ones, but also many bad ones. They all focus on accumulating money and gaining recognition for themselves.

"In our area, it seemed that the junior players would go searching from one club to another for a good coach. Amanda had her first instructor when she was eight years old, and she stayed with him for two years, having a lesson a week. After that period, she had no knowledge of what to do with a short ball, nor did she know about approach shots, or lobs. Instead of instruction, the pro would criticize and become sarcastic. So I decided to change.

"While I looked for a good pro, I enrolled Amanda in drill sessions at another club. She was still enthusiastic and always willing to practice. Other parents watching her group would comment that she was the only player who smiled, which encouraged me. Finally, one father recommended Dick Preston, a coach who not only enjoyed working with kids, but would watch them in tournament play too.

"Preston was indeed charismatic, and — at first — paid special attention to Amanda. She'd always hoped she'd have a private coach, and I think [she] felt Dick was the one. But I wasn't as sure. And my suspicions were proven correct when Shirley, a junior from another state, moved into our area and joined Preston's club. After a few months, his attention turned to her.

"Amanda felt jealous, I guess, and would compete with Shirley in drills. But if she won a point from Shirley, Preston would send Amanda to the last court to work with the ball machine for the rest of the session. He never let the two practice against each other. After two hours, Amanda would leave the court in tears. Yet she liked Preston, and wanted to stay in his group.

"I became convinced Preston wanted a junior he could mold, and control. I stood between him and Amanda, so my daughter got short shrift. But Shirley's parents eventually stopped paying for their lessons. Shirley spent more time at Preston's house than she did at her own, and her parents encouraged her to spend all her free time on the tennis court. Eventually, Amanda realized she would not become the coach's favorite. That broke her heart, but had she stayed with him much longer, she would have been seriously hurt emotionally.

"A few years later, we had the misfortune of meeting another teaching pro, a veteran of the women's pro circuit who'd just been hired at the local club. Amanda had recently spent two weeks at a Florida academy — which she loved and wanted to return to, but which we couldn't afford — and began to practice with the ex-pro.

"After awhile, Amanda's attitude changed. The woman was brainwashing her, playing psychological games and turning her against us. Amanda, meanwhile, was idolizing her.

"My husband and I decided we had to get Amanda out of that environment. So we took out a bank loan, and sent her to Florida. Amanda had the dream of playing professionally, and we shared her desire for success, but we didn't want her to be hurt. The teaching pros we encountered always seemed to want the money first, and made promises that reflected their interests ahead of Amanda's. But perhaps we simply never found the right person.

"In the end, Amanda received a full scholarship to a good university, and still enjoys tennis. She's talented, not burnt-out, and if she wishes to turn pro, she still can. But I learned that tennis is a tough, expensive sport, and that one must fight many things to survive and excel."

A CONTRACTUAL ARRANGEMENT

Parents should not hesitate to formalize their relationship with their child's coach. After all, the coach is more than likely going to put the child through a fairly serious evaluation before the child is taken on for private lessons.

(Clinic situations are, obviously, less formal. And the coach in those large groups won't have the same influence over a child's development.) Even John McEnroe passed through that phase, being put through a series of drills by Tony Palafox before being accepted into the prestigious Port Washington (New York) Tennis Academy program. (His nervous father had the late Chuck McKinley, an ex-United States Davis Cup star turned stockbroker, call Palafox for a straight, unguarded opinion of McEnroe's prospects following the 15-minute evaluation. Acceptable, Palafox told McKinley.)

"Every coach I know will do an evaluation," says Nick Bollettieri. "At our academy, we do between 50 and 60 evaluations a year. A parent will write or phone first to make an appointment, then bring the child in for a day, or two.

"When I conduct the evaluation," Bollettieri continues, "I look for three elements: desire to win, attitude, and—most importantly—footwork. I try to converse with the junior, to hear how he or she talks. 'I'm gonna work,' that's what I want to hear. 'I refuse to lose one point.' When Jimmy Arias first came for an evaluation, before I'd spent much time with him, I didn't think there was much future. Good high-school tennis, maybe college. But not a world-class champion. Then I listened to him, and realized he was a street fighter. Aaron Krickstein, in contrast, was more protected. He'd been sheltered by his family, watched over."

Whether a parent is signing his child on with a Bollettieri or a local pro, there are certain stipulations that ought to be agreed upon ahead of time. The coach ought to be able to insist upon a hands-off approach from the parent. If you want a great player, the coach is in effect saying, then I have some preconditions. If we're in agreement, fine. But if it isn't working out, then the agreement will have been violated and the relationship threatened. The coach should state that the parent is welcome to observe lessons, but not to criticize or provide additional instruction. The parent has to be willing to provide support to the coach's program: adequate equipment, transportation to tournaments, encouragement at home. In return, the parent ought to insist on a regular schedule of lessons, proper preparation for tournaments, and a perspective on the game that keeps pressure off and maintains enjoyment and fun.

Putting this into a document, signed by both parent and pro, is a good first step. And it should be followed up by regular meetings — perhaps one every six months — which would not be dissimilar to parent-teacher conferences. The coach, as teacher, can tell the parent not only how the child has performed, but how the parent has performed, too, and what the areas of potential problems or conflict are.

The school analogy ought to extend, too, to the parent-child relationship. A "report card" — photocopied and then filled out by the player on a monthly or bimonthly basis — can be the basis for an ongoing evaluation of the parental role. A sample report card (reproduced below) prepared by the Center for Athletic Excellence lists 12 different areas for grading (from A to F), including "Parent shares a healthy interest in my tennis" and "Parent doesn't try to be

REPORT CARD

Parent's Name _____

Athlete's Name _____

Reporting Period _____

This report card is designed to provide important feedback to parents on their effectiveness in dealing with their son's or daughter's competitive sport experience. Parents are performers, too. For the competitive sport experience of young children to be healthy and enriching, parents must *perform*.

This report card should be filled out by the child and submitted to the parent and coach every 2 to 3 months. A parent-coach conference should be held to discuss the report card results. A separate card is to be filled out for both parents.

Grading Categories:

A Excellent performance   D Poor performance
B Good performance   F Failure
C Average performance

_____ Parent shares a healthy interest in my tennis

_____ Parent doesn't put pressure on me to win

_____ Parent is supportive and encouraging about my tennis

_____ Parent doesn't make me feel guilty about the money and time being spent on my tennis

_____ Parent has a positive attitude about my tennis

_____ Parent helps me emotionally when I have hard or difficult times in my tennis

_____ Parent is not getting overinvolved in my tennis

_____ Parent looks very positive and relaxed during my matches

_____ Parent doesn't try to be my coach — he, she lets my pro do that

_____ Parent doesn't nag me for failure to play more tennis, do my exercises, running, and so forth

_____ Parent helps me to feel good about myself and my tennis

_____ Overall evaluation as a tennis parent

Suggestions: _____
_____
_____

_____
Date   *Signature of Athlete*

my coach—he/she lets my pro do that." Parents and children can use the report cards as vehicles for venting frustration. By talking about home and school life, the lines of communication stay open, and extraneous pressure is more easily avoided.

Just as the parent can help train the child, so can the child train his or her parent. Children who are successful in tennis tend to exhibit above-average intelligence. A survey conducted at the 1987 Easter Bowl championships in Miami indicated that less than 10 percent of 384 players there had less than a B average in school, and that an astonishing 99.4 percent planned to go to college. Structured feedback—through report cards or a similar vehicle—is a technique this group can comfortably handle.

OCCUPYING A PARENT'S FREE TIME

As a junior moves up the competitive ladder, the parent's on-court role diminishes. But the parent is still involved in almost every aspect of competitive play, from helping to arrange the child's schedule to chaperoning the junior to tournaments that may be hundreds of miles from home. Nothing can be more frustrating for a parent than to invest time and money in their junior's game and see the child lose to a player ranked well below him. And if that frustration is not disguised, its effect on the child can carry over and eventually contribute to burnout.

Charting is one way of controlling this frustration. A chart of a match can provide an objective review of what's gone on in competition, and it can highlight a child's strengths as well as weaknesses. (It's important to remember that parental observation, whether it's during a practice session or a match, does not have to be negative or critical of shortcomings. A positive response—finding the good in what may have been a bad situation—may accomplish more than any criticism.)

"Once a match is under way," Vic Braden noted in *Teaching Tennis to Children* on behalf of charting, "you can sit and watch as an interested spectator who applauds the good shots of both players—or you can play the role of a coach and 'scout' your child's performance." Percentage of first serves, number of unforced errors off the forehand and backhand, percentage of serves returned—all can be seen in an effective chart. And the charter will also be able to watch for intangibles like hustle, willingness to hit for winners and play aggressively, and whether the child tried to stick with a game plan.

"You'll be able to move past the final score," concluded Braden, "and talk positively about the match she played, thus reaffirming your insistence that the outcome of a match is only incidental to your interest in her tennis game."

A parent can create his own makeshift chart, drawing the outline of a tennis court on a piece of paper and using various symbols for shots—"fh" for forehand, "bh" for backhand, and so on. These tend to be inaccurate, however, and—at the higher levels of the game—have been supplanted by computerized forms that resemble the punch-out multiple-choice forms you may recall from your College Board test days. The best of these, Bollettieri Tenn-Stat

(PO Box 509262, Indianapolis, IN 46250), couples a point-by-point analysis of the match (each point requiring the parent to make six or seven pencil marks) with an emotion factoring. If a match chart indicates, after being run through the Tenn-Stat computer, that a child's emotional stability had a negative effect on the match's outcome, the parent is then sent a more complicated form to fill out in a subsequent match.

Coaches, particularly those who can't get to tournaments themselves, may ask parents to chart matches for specific shots. Or parents may offer to do so for coaches. If a parent can watch—and chart—a tournament match objectively, he can function as a coach's eyes and ears away from home.

Parents can also watch practice sessions, when convenient, but ought to resist taking notes. Neither the child nor the coach can fully communicate the interaction taking place on the court, and monitoring can give a parent a better sense of how the child is developing, and where the potential strengths and weaknesses lie. Exactly how this is to be done, however, ought to be worked out in advance, perhaps as a part of the contractual arrangement. Where the parent sits, when the parent and child should discuss the parent's observations, and when the coach and parent should meet are all aspects of the relationship to be worked out before the parent comes to the court.

Parents with too much time on their hands are a problem for tournaments, too. In the nine-state Southern section of the United States Tennis Association last year, seminars for parents and players were introduced at Mississippi's qualifying tournament for the national junior events, where, as

Jean Peabody, the chairwoman of the section's Education and Recreation Committee, said, "the pressure really begins for young, inexperienced kids." These seminars, in Jackson, Mississippi, featured a local sport psychologist, Dr. James Hollinsworth of the University of Southern Mississippi.

Although the seminar program is being extended through the Southern section, at most tournaments parents still fend for themselves. This is also true in most top-level junior programs, despite the pressure both parents and players are under. But, as in Mississippi, change is in the air. At the Nick Bollettieri Tennis Academy, for example, parents and players are regularly brought together for group discussions. And in the Bronx, New York, in the shadow of Yankee Stadium at the Stadium Tennis Club, family therapist David Rosenthal has begun a special group therapy for half the juniors in Stadium's elite tournament program.

In 1984, the support group began, hesitantly. Stadium's tennis director saw it as a once-a-week experiment, 45 minutes of talk between workouts. For the half-dozen teenagers, ranging from 13 to 16, it was a novelty, too. Most had never had the opportunity to sit with their peers and talk about not only their on-court frustrations, but their off-court ones as well.

"It was hard at first," recalled Rosenthal, who'd been a therapist for ten years and a teaching pro for three when the group began. "But eventually they helped each other."

For several, the biggest issue they faced was their parents' wishes and dreams. Finally, Rosenthal realized he had to involve the parents, too.

"The parents were so hooked up in their children's tennis" Rosenthal said, "but many of them hadn't talked about their own experiences with the children. In the group, one confessed he'd been given a scholarship to play college tennis, then broke his leg before his freshman year and had it taken away. Another admitted he'd gotten a major-league tryout as a shortstop, and failed.

"We could feel the relief among the kids. This wasn't just a game to the parents. They hadn't been able to tolerate the losses, the slow development of a backhand. Now, getting this out, they became more tolerant of their children being children. The kids were able to be in more of a peak performance state."

Rosenthal won't go so far as to say the win-loss records dramatically improved. There were other influences, too, including excellent coaching and facilities. But the discussions didn't hurt.

Giving the parents a chance to talk, to interact, and to participate, Rosenthal concluded, kept tennis in perspective.

7 JUNIOR DEVELOPMENT: WHY IT ISN'T WORKING WELL

At the 1986 Masters tournament at New York City's Madison Square Garden, the eight men designated as the world's best for that calendar year gathered for one final, king-of-the-hill confrontation. Not one was an American, the product of junior tennis in the United States. Three came from Sweden, two from France, another from Ecuador, a tiny South American country with fewer players than a Californian or Floridian city. One finalist came from West Germany. The other grew up in Czechoslovakia. It was small solace that Ivan Lendl, the Masters champion, now lives in southern Connecticut, for he, like women's champion Martina Navratilova, is a product of a junior tennis system that—like Sweden's, France's, and Germany's programs—is quite unlike the United States'.

No, that Navratilova and Lendl have moved here to reap the benefits of their tennis talent is small comfort to the United States Tennis Association and its patrons. There are few Americans on the horizon to challenge them— John McEnroe on the men's side, perhaps Pam Shriver on the women's—and their heirs appear to be European.

Despite the hundreds of thousands of dollars poured into American junior tennis by sponsors such as PepsiCo, Merrill Lynch, Rolex, Ellesse, Rossignol, Penn, Prince, Head, Nike, and scores of other equipment and clothing manufacturers, the American system is producing few players who can consistently win at the highest levels of world-class competition. Indeed, many of the most promising American juniors are burning out and giving up the game long before they reach that heady level.

"In junior tennis, the United States has the talent," insists Nick Bollettieri. "You take the top 15 boys, the top 15 girls, and no country can beat us. Any criticism about talent is unwarranted. The talent exists."

Yet in the box scores—major championships, Davis Cup, the international junior events—the United States has not performed well. If there's anything to blame, it must be the system.

A QUICK COMPARISON

Canadian tennis official and coach Joseph Brabenec, currently training the South Korean national squad, surveyed the top European systems recently when his country was contemplating underwriting a program to develop elite juniors. His findings show that Sweden, Czechoslovakia, and France—unlike the United States—share a tremendous emphasis on league play, coupled with a national coaching system that automatically promotes juniors to more sophisticated levels of coaching. The juniors and their families are spared the psychological anguish of having to dismiss old coaches and find new ones. They're also spared the great expenses of lessons and court fees: in all three countries, both are subsidized by the national federations.

Exactly how significant a difference have this attitude and support made? Compare the numbers of Europeans and Americans on the men's pro tour. In 1982, the United States had 37 men in the world's top 100 players, and another 35 in the next 100. Europe had 30 and 29, respectively, a total of 59 to the United States' 72. (The remainder came from South America, Australia, New Zealand, Asia, and Africa.) Just three and a half years later, in August 1986, the relationship had reversed itself. Europe could boast 39 in the top 100, and the United States just 32. More significantly, the European community's depth was shown by the second 100: here, Europeans claimed 42 spots on the computer list, while Americans took but 22.

Brabenec's research into the top tennis-elite developmental systems unearthed some interesting statistics. Generally, elite players take between seven and ten years to develop, regardless of the country. Of the four countries, Czechoslovakia has the fewest facilities—just 600 clubs with a total of 1,500 courts. But virtually all these clubs have elite (or tournament-level) junior programs, which members help run (not surprisingly, given the socialist society

Czechs live in; indeed, members pitch in to build new courts as well). Sweden has more clubs, roughly 1,000, but only 600 run junior programs. In Sweden, these local programs are coached by "amateurs" who receive a subsidy from the government for each 40-minute lesson. The lessons average five students and the students are charged three dollars. France has by far the largest European facility pool—more than 6,500 clubs—and a unique arrangement for juniors: the country's schoolchildren have a holiday every Wednesday, and the tennis clubs hold special clinics on that day.

All three countries have a national federation that oversees both regional and local associations. Here's a country-by-country rundown.

Sweden. Sweden's 23 tennis regions organize three or four training camps annually for a region's top 13- and 14-year-olds. The cream of that crop—as many as one dozen juniors 14 or under—is invited to one of six "super-regions" training camps, which are underwritten by the national association. And once a year, in May, the 56 top boys and girls under 14 are invited to Bastad for a one-week camp, and another 24 to 30 older juniors (up to 18) go to a national elite camp. That latter group makes up the core of the country's international traveling junior squad, which gets a huge chunk of the national federation budget: Brabenec estimates 70 percent, or more.

Junior tournaments are strictly limited, particularly at the national level. The competitions are held on three levels—local, regional, and countrywide—but only two players from a given region are invited to the five annual national events. Much of the play is in junior and senior interclub leagues, and there's a strong sense of support for emerging juniors among fellow club members. Nationally, the federation encourages this kind of talent scouting: a program named Donald Duck holds an annual tournament in three age groups. Six years ago, the tournament attracted 13,000 players under 15; a decade earlier, when it began, only 1,400 children played in its draw.

Like the tournaments, there are three levels of Swedish tennis coaches, too. And in 1985, the federation instituted an academy at Bastad for the country's top 14 boys and girls over 14.

Birger Folke, a national coach, once suggested to a reporter that the emphasis on local clubs gave players more court time. "We have good facilities and good pros in small towns," Folke told the *International Tennis Weekly*, "and players there can play a lot of matches. They can play in the junior team and in the senior team. In the small towns, they get more practice hours than they would in large cities. Then when they get to be 15 or 16, they must go to the big cities to play against the best players."

Even the Swedes concede, however, that to reach the pinnacle, they had to go outside their boundaries. After Siab, the wealthy Swedish construction firm, agreed to underwrite a national touring team, the first thing Jon-Anders Sjogren did with his newfound funding was to buy a bunch of plane tickets to Australia.

"We had to try to teach them more volleys, to be more aggressive," he explained. And, needless to say, they succeeded.

Czechoslovakia. The Czech tennis tradition is, today, about as influential as professional football's was in the United States in the seventies—in other words, all-encompassing. The country, with only 60,000 registered tennis-club members, claims the best male and female players in the world, and several contenders for both crowns.

Elite junior programs are found at almost every one of the nation's 600 clubs, and each is run by one or two volunteer coaches who are minimally compensated. Competition focuses on league play. There are five national leagues, or divisions, and each senior six-player team (four men and two women) must have two junior members (a boy and a girl). Hana Mandlikova recalls that a Czech club's coach always has to make himself available when the team's members want to practice. That's not surprising, given that a club's federation funding often is based on how well it's doing in league play.

In addition to the leagues, there are nearly 200 junior tournaments annually, and seven national and regional training centers. The federation administers skill and fitness tests for the centers, and parental approval is, of course, also required before a junior is accepted. At the centers, no more than ten players will be working daily. And from those, the national federation chooses up to four from each age group to play in the international junior events.

Like the Swedes, the Czechs believe in national talent scouting. Their annual open junior event attracts approximately 10,000 players. And the intensity the youngsters bring to the game is a product, many Westerners suspect, of the Communist system they live under. Tennis success gives Czechs an opportunity to travel with unusual freedom and, since the departure of Navratilova, to keep whatever prizes they may win, including money. Add to that the fact that the Czechs are oppressed, and have learned — almost as a race — to keep their own counsel, and you have juniors who've learned mental toughness long before the topspin backhand.

"I know I'm different," Ivan Lendl confessed to *Tennis Magazine* before the 1986 United States Open, "but I don't think people understand that I went through very difficult times when I started playing because my background is more — *different* — than anyone here can imagine. In Czechoslovakia, for example, you live with your parents until you get married and, even then, you probably live with one set of parents because you have no other place to live. Can you imagine living with your mother-in-law?"

It's almost as tough as imagining a country with only 60,000 tennis players dominating the world.

France. The historical tradition of world-class tennis here starts earlier than in either Sweden or Czechoslovakia, beginning in the twenties with Rene Lacoste and the other "Musketeers" and Suzanne Lenglen. And the string, through Yannick Noah and Henri Leconte, is almost unbroken. It's not surprising, then, that Brabenec concludes the French Tennis Federation "is the best organized in the world, with more commercial and social influence in the country's private clubs than [national federations have] in either Sweden or Czechoslovakia."

The French federation oversees thirty national and six overseas club leagues and an ongoing talent identification program. Early junior instruction is given at the club level, and elite players are singled out and nurtured at seven regional and five national training centers. The former are funded by the federation and the respective regional association, the latter by the federation and the French government. All centers are staffed by full-time coaches, and recruitment begins at age 14. At each center, there are usually no more than 14 juniors, and these group sessions are augmented by private clinics. In 1986, the French completed still another center at Stade Roland Garros, the Parisian complex that hosts the French Open.

Perhaps most significant is the French junior ranking system. Rather than recognizing a relative handful of players, as the United States lists do, the French use a handicap system to rank up to 5,000 annually.

The passion the French bring to the game may ultimately be a drawback in world-class competition, however. Brabenec found that the best players can become wealthy through French wins and endorsements alone. Becoming number one, he concluded, was not a priority for success. At least not in France.

ON THE HOME FRONT

In the United States, there are 17 sectional associations affiliated with the United States Tennis Association, but virtually all of the thousands of tennis clubs are private. Since the USTA puts few of its funds back into these clubs, its influence on their operation is minimal. Moreover, because these clubs must be self-supporting, they tend to emphasize the kind of recreational play and instruction that suit the broadest cross section of their membership.

The independence of the private club makes it difficult for the USTA to implement a national elite development program on the European model. To date, elite development has been in the hands of a small group of coaches, the best known being the late Harry Hopman, Vic Braden, Dennis Van der Meer, and Nick Bollettieri. Their efforts are supported by the emergence of a strong collegiate tennis program: current estimates have 1,500 colleges doling out $57 million worth of scholarships annually, with most of the major schools having five scholarships available per team per year. (This, however, is a bone of contention. University of California at Irvine coach Greg Patton has called for either uniformity in scholarships—with all schools having the same number—or their abolition. Players, Patton complained to *Tennis U.S.A.*, "think a scholarship is a ranking.")

Beyond college, the USTA matches the Europeans, paying for national Junior Davis Cup, Wightman Cup, and Federation Cup teams. But between learning at the grassroots level—where the USTA has recently put a strong effort into its Schools Program—and college, there is not much in the way of a national development program. And college, with its four-year limit on coaching, and its requirement that athletes pay equal attention to their studies, is not an environment likely to build a world-class player. While the Swedes, the Czechs, and the French are playing international matches, the American juniors are trapped in a national pressure cooker of age-group rankings, and are, for the most part, developing limited games on hard courts, the surface on which all major United States championships are currently held.

Dennis Van der Meer has echoed this last observation, noting that one recent men's computer list showed only five American-reared (and so hardcourt-reared) players in the world's top 20. The rest, except for South African-turned-American Johan Kriek, learned their games on clay. Other criticism has emerged, too. For the past 70 years, noted *Tennis Week* publisher Eugene Scott, a former American Davis Cupper, the junior tournament format has remained unchanged. Individual sections designate which players are eligible for national events, and those choices can occasionally be politically motivated. Moreover, although sections vary markedly in the quality of their youngsters' play, a minimum number from each are required to be accepted in the draw of every major USTA junior event. (Technically speaking, that's *junior* meaning all boys and girls; as far as the USTA is concerned, *junior* is a term that applies only to 18-and-under events, not the other age groups.) Nor has the USTA—despite the money it currently earns from the highly profitable United States Open—seen fit to hire national coaches, or to open a full-time, free training facility for elite juniors. Scott's solutions would include regional coaches and centers to which juniors would be brought for a month or two, more competitive play during the summer months, and continued emphasis on the Schools Program.

What is the Schools Program? Launched in 1984 on a trial basis in Florida, the program is an attempt to create large introductory tennis classes in public schools, whether they've got tennis courts or not. The Florida program began under the direction of Barbara Braunstein, a teaching pro from New Jersey, who once arrived at a USTA seminar carrying pizza, flowers, and an Easter basket; all, she explained, were tools of her trade—recruiting volunteers to work with specific schools. Braunstein made even more of an impact when she brought tennis to the 60 schoolchildren at the Miccosukee Indian reservation in the Florida Everglades. One week after she'd visited, and left behind 20 donated racquets and 100 balls, the Miccosukees held their first tournament.

Although it's hard to imagine a future American champion coming out of the Florida swamps, or off the inner-city sidewalks—the expense of the game would seem to prohibit that—the USTA is ecstatic over the program's grass-roots success. In the three years the Schools Program has been in operation, coordinator Larry Tabak estimates, nearly 2 million children (the program is focused on fifth- and sixth-graders) have learned the game. The USTA has spent almost $1 million in this effort and has enlisted volunteers at each school to teach the eight-lesson curriculum. The list of cities and towns scheduled to join the program in the fall of 1986 gives a sense of the reach: Waterloo, Iowa; Lincoln, Nebraska; Las Vegas; Burlington, Vermont; Austin, Texas; and Baltimore. In Atlanta alone, Tabak estimates, 8,000 schoolchildren were exposed to the game.

But for development purposes, the Schools Program doesn't do much. Ideally, municipal summer programs on courts in city and suburban public parks could reap the benefits (the evidence is mixed on this to date). But the private clubs—where the professional teaching and coaching is available—are not formally tied in. And given that the United States already has 25 million of the earth's 55 million tennis players, it's clear that sheer numbers don't correspond with competitive success.

Tabak conceded as much to *World Tennis* magazine.

"I don't think you logically get better tennis players from having more tennis players," he said. "Our role is to get all those kids interested in tennis, and if some of them decide to take the game seriously, that's great. But I'd rather see that out of 100 kids, 99 of them are still playing when they're 40."

SOME RECOMMENDATIONS FOR FURTHER CHANGE

For parents whose children are becoming competitive tennis players, the future of the junior game will affect their pocketbook, their role, and their relationships with their children.

Dramatic changes could reduce individual parents' costs, particularly if some system of subsidized coaching is begun. A more systematized approach to evaluating talent could lessen the political nature of sectional rankings and endorsements for national tournaments. In the best of all worlds, a national elite program could create selfless—rather than selfish—role models, a step every parent at every level would give thanks for.

But will it happen?

Debate is already well under way within the USTA over how to implement an elite junior program in the United States. Should there be a national academy? National coaches? How should the selection process work? Should the tournament structure be revamped? What can be done to cope with burnout and the extreme pressure top juniors find themselves under?

Where to start is a problem. One recent USTA meeting included the following proposals on its agenda: a national training center; new emphasis on team play; new coordination with interscholastic tennis; the elimination or de-emphasis of rankings; additional levels of play, including regional, novice, and intermediate divisions; new tournament formats, including round-robins. None of the above could be fully agreed upon.

Nevertheless, there are some immediate steps that could be taken in several areas, innovative initiatives that would help parents and players deal with the stress of tennis both on and off the court.

First, the USTA, in conjunction with the USPTR and the USPTA, ought to offer specialized training for coaches and parents. The thrust of this effort would be to train coaches to help parents do a better job. Group discussion, for one, is a process alien to most coaches. Yet parents need such discussions to prepare themselves for competition. The seminars Seena Hamilton has begun holding at the annual Easter Bowl tournament are an example of how the system can comfortably integrate a concept like this. But the USTA hasn't pushed for it on a national basis yet.

With the support of the two teaching-pro associations, the parent-coach discussion groups could become part of any agreement made prior to a teaching professional taking on the responsibility of producing an elite player. A parents' workbook, a report card such as we described in the previous chapter, could be aspects of this training and part of the regular discussion.

The formalization of this parent-coach relationship would set a precedent that could extend beyond tennis and into all sport.

Second, the age-group requirements in junior tennis have to be changed. Children currently compete in four formal groups: 12-and-under, 14-and-under, 16-and-under, and 18-and-under. But eligibility to play in a given group is dictated arbitrarily, by whether one's birthday falls before or after January 1 of a given calendar year. A significant number of children are put at a disadvantage by an "unlucky" birthday and are forced up into an older division before a ranking season is concluded. For younger children, a year can have profound physical implications, and 12-year-olds who must play others nearly 15 are no more likely to fare well than Little Leaguers going against the Babe Ruth League.

The USTA, instead, ought to allow juniors to play in their own age group until they're too old. Simple enough, right? Except that Australia used that rule for years, then was ordered to revert to an arbitrary calendar date by the International Tennis Federation. If the ITF won't bend, the USTA could give players the option of moving up or staying where they are until their real birthdays. Such a change would eliminate the inherent pressure of bad birthdays and give juniors and parents more control over the child's development.

Third, the early competition age groups—the 12-and-under and the 14-and-under divisions (and, of course, the 10-and-unders in those sections where competition begins that early)—should focus on team, rather than individual, participation. Even in the 16s and 18s, the USTA should make an effort to encourage team play. In some states, Texas for one, interscholastic tennis attracts more students than basketball; one Texas daily newspaper ranks more than 100 teams on a week-to-week basis. In many other states, it's all but invisible.

Team tennis is valuable. It teaches one to be a part of a larger unit, helps to build peer relationships, is a natural source of motivation, and teaches one to be bigger than one's self. For young kids, being on a team can take pressure off. For older players, an esprit de corps can generate positive on-court emotions. The Swedish men prove that.

Fourth, the USTA should eliminate national rankings below the 14-and-under group. The ITF has already banned 12-and-under international tournaments and world rankings. If the sections insist on retaining regional rankings in the 12s, so be it. But team play could easily be substituted here for national individual tournaments, allowing juniors the travel experience and the competition without the pressure of rankings and what-if-I-lose.

Fifth, the United States has to create a national development program, a system that lifts the economic burden off individual families and allows relatively equal opportunity for all top juniors. At the moment, the bridges needed to move from one level to the next aren't in place. The grass-roots effort in the schools is fine. But from that point on, there is virtually nothing on a national basis until a player has achieved high status (invitations to national clinics, free clothing and equipment from manufacturers).

Without a coaching system, without the means to identify children with special talents and needs, such a system can't be put in place. As good as the USPTA and the USPTR are, they are not complete models. They have established their own standards, which reflect their members' backgrounds. Coaches at the highest level need special training in exercise physiology, nutritional science, sport psychology, biomechanics, and advanced coaching. Presently, the USPTA and USPTR concentrate their testing on playing and teaching skills, the history of the sport, and business acumen, such as whether the coach can run a pro shop. A national system needs more depth.

There has to be financial support, too. European juniors are permitted to play professional events and to keep whatever money they win without jeopardizing their standing in their country's junior rankings. Americans, obviously, are not. Not only would they lose amateur status in the USTA's eyes, they would also be in trouble as far as the NCAA is concerned for college tennis. That support, in whatever shape it takes, has to facilitate a successful junior's rise through the ranks. If a player is winning at the local level, he should be able to play comfortably at the sectional level, regardless of the expense. And he should be able to move to national events if successful in the region. Money should, literally, be no object.

National coaches should be hired and given specific groups of juniors to be responsible for. They should have budgets funded by the USTA, but under their control. And they should have access to training centers, ideally one of several regional facilities. If a junior wants to stay with his private coach, fine. But no one should fall through the cracks.

The regional training centers should, of course, be spread around the country. Every successful junior should have access to one regional site, and the top players at those centers should feed into an elite program at a central site. This program would include the players who currently make up the junior teams playing international matches. And it would serve as the research center (see the next recommendation) where the computer and its information, as well as the development program's administration, would be housed.

Obviously, this plan wouldn't come cheap. But using existing facilities, perhaps the Olympic training center in Colorado Springs, could cut the costs.

Finally, in conjunction with a national development program, the USTA should launch an ongoing national research program, using the players in the national elite group for study purposes. The private-academy setting has already given some insight into strategies for reducing on-court pressure in an away-from-home environment. At the Bollettieri academy, for example, we found that weekly massage sessions gave young players a sense of security and relaxation that they typically would get when hugged at home. Other questions—what are too many hours on the court? What's the best way to warm up to prevent injury? What's the best way to educate parents, and when? What are the effects of competitive stress at various levels in various age groups? What is the effect of academy life — have yet to be answered.

A national computer system could tie into the development network, tracking juniors, identifying problems as soon as they crop up, perhaps discovering their sources as well. Without such a system, tracking talent will be extremely difficult.

Ultimately, the goal of such a national development program would be to take the burden of development off the parents. The guilt a child feels when the sport consumes so much of the family's money and time will lessen. And the USTA will be able to influence the development of a proper role model as never before. This, in turn, will generate a sense of loyalty toward the national organization. "What has the USTA ever done for me?" has been the attitude of many players, and it's carried some truth: the parents have picked up the tab, chosen the coaches, and provided the player's support system. With a national development program, the USTA once and for all will become a powerful, positive force for all levels of American tennis.

And parents, players, and teaching professionals will all be the stronger for it.

Epilogue

Mark was nine years old and a precocious player. To his parents, he seemed blessed with exceptional natural talent, and — in his state age-group tournaments at any rate — he was already beating older, more experienced players.

But although his game appeared older than his years, there were other aspects to Mark's on-court behavior that weren't as mature. In the middle of a match, whether he was behind or ahead, Mark would begin weeping. Embarrassed, he'd lose several points, and rarely regain his composure completely. Across the net, his opponents would uncomfortably avert their eyes. On the sidelines, his parents would try to figure out what had gone wrong.

For a year, Mark's parents struggled with the dilemma. First they pulled their son out of the league matches he'd been playing. They talked about stress, telling him no sport was important enough to weep over at his age. When that had little effect, they tried ignoring the sobs, letting him play through them. That didn't stem the flow either.

Mark's parents were convinced that tennis was no longer fun for their son, and they told him it was time to stop competing, at least for awhile. Mark refused. It would be punishment to put down his racquet, he complained. Making him give up the game would not be doing him any favors, he said.

A month later, Mark's parents reluctantly allowed him to play a 12-and-under event in a city not too far from their home. Mark's older sister was entered in the 14s, and there was no 10-and-under division. Besides, Mark was adamant that he wanted to play.

His mother recalled what happened. "We carefully defined what was acceptable behavior, and he agreed to try it," she remembered. "He successfully beat his first opponent with no crying, only to face the number-one seed in the next round. Mark played him even up at 4–4 in the first set, and then the tears appeared as he lost several crucial points, due to his shot selection. He lost the set 6–4.

"After the first set, the match was over, Mark losing 6–1 in the second set. During the match, Mark appeared to be trying to control his emotions, taking time to retrieve the ball and resume play."

But even the control hadn't worked. With reddened eyes, Mark agreed that he wasn't ready for tournament play, despite his talent, despite his fundamentally winning attitude. Then, the pressure off, he won the tournament's consolation round.

There are no surefire formulas to becoming a successful tennis parent, no shortcuts, no tricks of the trade. Each child, each junior player is different, and a parent trained for competition quickly learns that a match record top-heavy with wins does not automatically translate into a trouble-free path for emotional development.

Different parents develop different strategies for coping with the burden of competition, but those who cope best keep the pressure off their children. Those parents bring their children into the game, then pull back, turning the coaching over to others with greater expertise. They are supportive, but not domineering; attentive, but not using their children as athletic surrogates.

And, in the end, they are constantly reminding themselves that the essence of the game — its true value, its enduring quality — is of the moment: the strings singing sweetly as the ball is struck, the squeak of the sneaker sliding into position, the wit and intelligence of a disguised lob or drop shot, the sweat, the effort, the experience.

There are few pots of gold at the end of a tennis career, so few as to be statistically insignificant. It is today that tennis parents must focus upon, not tomorrow, or next ranking period, or next age group. And it is *this* day that parents must be able to say to themselves: if my child never plays again, this experience will have taught him a wonderful lesson. Tennis will have helped him grow, and become a better person.

For nine-year-old Mark, tennis was not working. And he was lucky. His parents recognized it was healthier for him to walk away from the court now than to press forward and face greater risks later. For hundreds of Marys and Johns, the stress has not been relieved. Yet it is in the stress-free, pressure-free environment that the best tennis, winning tennis, is played.

Control, consistency, perspective.

If there is a formula for success in junior tennis, for success, in fact, in any sport, then *that* is it.

And the trained tennis parent understands.